THE LEGEND OF JOHNNY THUNDERS

Looking For Johnny

Danny Garcia

Foreword by Stevie Klasson

Introduction by Nina Antonia

Punk ★ Hostage ★ Press

Looking For Johnny
Danny Garcia
ISBN 978-1-940213-03-3

All interviews conducted by Danny Garcia,
except Billy Rath by Simon Ritt and Peter Perrett by Nina Antonia.
Transcripts by Daisy Wake for Flo Globe Productions.
Edited by Nina Antonia

Cover photograph by Marcia Resnick
Portrait of Johnny by Jimmy Angelina/JimmyAngelina.com

Photographs courtesy of Marcia Resnick, Yann Mercader, Phyllis Stein,
Patrick Grandperret, Xavi Mercadé.

Edited for publication
Wyatt Doyle
Danny Garcia   Iris Berry

Introduction
Nina Antonia

Foreword
Stevie Klasson

Design
Wyatt Doyle

Punk Hostage Press, Hollywood, USA, www.punkhostagepress.com

Contents

Foreword

I made a decision many years ago not to do any interviews about Johnny Thunders; I made him a promise just before he died that I was gonna live off my own talent. Now a lot of people who jammed with Johnny for five minutes use that as their claim to fame, and I never wanted to be one of them.

The other reason being that we were really close; Johnny was like the older brother that I never had, and most interviewers just wanted to dig up dirt and talk about his drug addiction. (I made the mistake of giving an interview with that Lech Kallopski [sic] for that horrible movie he made before I realized what he was doing. Luckily, my lawyer managed to pull me out of that one. Bless him.)

The myth of Johnny Thunders and the real Johnny Thunders I knew and loved were pretty far apart. I'm also really close to his family, and I don't want to contribute to any of this sickening crap. His grandchildren don't need to hear that stuff. Johnny was a great guy in my book.

Any hoot, I've known Danny Garcia since the '90s, when he played bass with The Crybabys, and he is a dear friend and a stand-up guy. So when he called me to tell me he was making a Thunders movie, my first reaction was, *What kind of movie are you making?* He told me he wanted to wanted to talk to the people who were close to him, and make a movie about who Johnny really was. Now this put things into another perspective. I think he has done a good job of it, and it's the best portrait of Johnny so far. He has got my blessing.

It's still painful for me to talk about Johnny; I miss him so much. I see his grandkids all the time, and one day I'm gonna tell them about this amazing cat who was their grandfather who changed the course of rock 'n' roll. I was lucky to have known him and to have had him as a close friend. Life will never be the same.

One love.

STEVIE KLASSON, September 2015

Introduction

The restless spirit of rock 'n' roll, Johnny Thunders is now as much of an icon as James Dean or Jesse James. From the moment he took to the stage with the New York Dolls, who made their live debut at the tail-end of 1972, Thunders cut like a knife in a blur of squawking riffs, platform boots, and a chaotic bouffant that resembled a nest of unruly ravens. Possessed of a jagged grace, Johnny reinvented classic rock 'n' roll, fashioning a crash collage of Eddie Cochran meets Hubert Sumlin to create an inimitable going-off-the-rails guitar signature. From glam to punk, Thunders nabbed the rock 'n' roll essence of the 1950s and brought it screeching into the new era. His influence on countless generations of bands is virtually unquantifiable, as is his style and attitude.

A good boy turned "bad," but who never lost his heart, Thunders was lured by the temptations of the seamier side of the American night and was for many years marginalized by the mainstream because of his drug issues, but maintained a legion of devotees on both sides of the Atlantic, who could look beyond mean judgment. Why Johnny should have been made a junk scapegoat when many of his equally narcotized contemporaries weren't has more to do with his inability or refusal to play industry games. But this didn't stop him being one of the hardest working men in rock 'n' roll. Without major label support, he had no choice but to keep gigging. If you missed it, too bad; if you were too young, that's really too bad. However, thanks to Danny Garcia, we now have a worthy document in *Looking For Johnny*.

It is a testament to Danny's passion for Johnny that he dared to tread with compassion and empathy where others, aiming for a more sensational angle, have failed. The evidence of the eternal devotion of Johnny's fans was borne out by the community funding of *Looking For Johnny*, in a campaign that was led by Jerry Nolan's long-term companion, Phyllis Stein. A documentary about Johnny Thunders was not going to come from the music business establishment, and yet the enthusiasm with which *Looking*

For Johnny was received speaks volumes about how important the subject matter is.

As well as discovering Johnny's story and his legacy, Danny Garcia also captured the voices of those that knew him, conducting interviews with the likes of Alan Vega, Marcia Resnick, Frank Infante, Walter Lure, Gail Higgins, and Sylvain Sylvain, amongst others. Sadly, since the documentary was made in 2014, Leee Black Childers, Marty Thau, and Billy Rath have gone to the great midnight. The stories and anecdotes contained in this book are ever more precious, down for the record, a strike against mortality and a lasting testament to the inimitable spirit of Mr. Johnny Thunders, and stand as a worthy companion to the documentary.

NINA ANTONIA, August 2015

Nina Antonia is the author of Johnny Thunders…In Cold Blood *and* Too Much Too Soon: The New York Dolls.

Cast of Characters

In no way do the following brief descriptions constitute biographies of everyone who so kindly shared their memories in Looking for Johnny, *nor does it seek to quantify the depth of their association, but simply places them at the scene of involvement with Mr. Thunders.*

RACHEL AMODEO — NY-based filmmaker. Writer and director of *What About Me*, featuring Johnny Thunders and Jerry Nolan.

NINA ANTONIA — Writer. Penned Johnny's authorized biography, *Johnny Thunders...In Cold Blood*, first published in 1987.

NITE BOB — Sound man for Aerosmith, Iggy and the Stooges, and the New York Dolls.

LEEE BLACK CHILDERS — Photographer, Warholite, MainMan minder for David Bowie and Iggy Pop. Lee also managed The Heartbreakers.

TERRY CHIMES — Original drummer for The Clash. He guested with The Heartbreakers.

DONNA DESTRI — Singer and habitué of downtown NYC in its finest hours. Worked at Max's Kansas City.

BP FALLON — Rock 'n' roll singer and sage, publicist to Led Zeppelin and T. Rex. Manager of Johnny during recording of *So Alone*.

LINDA FALZARANO — Cousin of Lori Coleman, who dated Johnny in 1968.

ALISON GORDY — Singer. Vocalist with Johnny's backing band, The Oddballs.

BOB GRUEN — Photographer. Documented the New York Dolls on video.

GAIL HIGGINS — The Heartbreakers' assistant manager, and a personal friend of Johnny Thunders.

STEVE HOOKER — Guitarist with The Rumble and The Shakers. Also recorded with Levi Dexter.

FRANK INFANTE — Guitarist, formerly of Blondie. Infante also played with Iggy Pop and the latter-day New York Dolls.

BARRY JONES — Guitarist. Played with both The London Cowboys and Johnny Thunders.

PETER JORDAN — Bassist, roadie and stand-in for Arthur Kane in the New York Dolls.

TIMO KALTIO — Guitarist, bassist. Roadie for Hanoi Rocks and bassist for The Cherry Bombz. Toured with Johnny Thunders.

LENNY KAYE — Guitarist with Patti Smith Group. Cultural historian.

STEVIE KLASSON — Guitarist. Played with Johnny in The Oddballs.

RICHARD LLOYD — Guitarist. Played with Television.

WALTER LURE — Guitarist with The Heartbreakers. Recorded *L.A.M.F.* and toured extensively with Johnny Thunders.

CHRIS MUSTO — Drummer. Played with Johnny in The Oddballs.

PETER ORR — New Orleans artist. Brother of Jimmy Orr, friend of Johnny's.

JOHN PERRY — Guitarist with The Only Ones. Played with Johnny and contributed to *Que Sera Sera* and *Copy Cats*.

PETER PERRETT — Rhythm guitarist and The Only Ones' frontman. Contributed to *So Alone* and played with Johnny.

HOWIE PYRO — Bassist and DJ, played with D-Generation and The Blessed. Friend of Johnny Thunders.

BILLY RATH — Bassist with The Heartbreakers. Recorded *L.A.M.F.*, toured extensively with Johnny.

MARCIA RESNICK — Photographer and personal friend of Johnny.

RICK RIVETS — Guitarist for Actress and the first lineup of the New York Dolls.

SIMON RITT — Drummer. Played with The Daughters, recorded live tracks with Johnny.

CYNTHIA ROSS — Bassist. Formerly of The B-Girls, now playing with New York Junk.

LUIGI SCORCIA — Guitarist and bassist. Toured with Johnny and Jerry Nolan.

ANDY SHERNOFF — Bass, guitar and vocals with The Dictators. Attended same school as Johnny Thunders.

PHYLLIS STEIN — Worked at Max's Kansas City. Jerry Nolan's long-term companion.

SYLVAIN SYLVAIN — Guitarist in the New York Dolls.

MARTY THAU — Manager of the New York Dolls.

NEAL X — Guitarist with Sigue Sigue Sputnik and The Montecristos. Toured with Johnny.

SAMI YAFFA — Bassist with Hanoi Rocks and latter-day New York Dolls.

JILL WISOFF — Bassist with The Oddballs. Toured with Johnny.

FROM *Mona et moi*

Queens

NINA ANTONIA: Johnny was born in Queens, one of New York's outer boroughs, on July 15th, 1952, to Emile and Josephine Genzale. Emile Genzale was a bit of a ladykiller, and he left when Johnny was an infant.

SYLVAIN SYLVAIN: Poor Johnny. He called me in the 1980s and said, "My father passed away." And I said, "Oh I'm sorry, Johnny." And he says, "I don't give a fuck!" He had a rough time with his dad. His dad totally forgot about the whole family until Johnny started to make it and we were playing out in Queens. We were playing the Coventry, with Kiss and the Ramones opening up for us. [Emile] had remarried. He looked just like Johnny, by the way—very handsome, beautiful hair—and now he has his new wife and kids. They were all sweet, but it broke Johnny's heart when they were growing up together and he left his mother. There was always a void there that affected Johnny, through everything that he did.

MARTY THAU: Johnny came from a dysfunctional family, and his sister, Mariann, had great control over him. I believe he rebelled against that. Only when he started with the New York Dolls and she saw that he could do some recordings did she then realize, *Hmm, maybe this kid is on the right path.* She was not—to me anyway—the friendliest person.

ANDY SHERNOFF: I went to elementary school—PS 148—in the 1960s with Johnny Genzale. I lived around the corner on 88th Street and Northern. Johnny lived down on 83rd Street. They were great times, very innocent times. It was before The Beatles, even. At school we'd play stickball.

The neighborhood hasn't changed. None of the buildings have changed. I wasn't in Johnny's class, but I played sports with him after school. I have great memories of growing up in this area. It was safe. You could ride your bike in the streets. Muggings, robberies never occurred. Drugs? Didn't even know what drugs were.

Then, of course, The Beatles came along and changed my life and changed Johnny's life and we knew the best way to get girls—the best way to have fun—was playing rock 'n' roll.

JILL WISOFF: I can only say that baseball was his passion as a kid and he wanted to be a pro baseball player. That was his thing, but he ended up going into music. I read later that he couldn't do Little League because he needed his father to bring him. He had the shoulders for a baseball player. He was a little guy, but you could definitely see that.

GAIL HIGGINS: Mariann had turned him on to 1950s music and the girl groups. That was the similarity between him, my cousin, and myself—we all had aunts and uncles or sisters or brothers who all were into 1950s music, and we were all listening to that.

LINDA FALZARANO: My cousin-in-law, Lori Coleman (now Lori Coleman Connelly), used to date Johnny in 1968. They were in 11th grade and were very much in love, like maybe puppy love. He had a band at the time called The Reign. They had a great time, but if [Lori] would do something that he didn't like, it would be the end of the world. She told me one time she went to a Hendrix concert. She went with—not even another guy, just a girlfriend—and [Johnny] met her after the show. They took a walk over a bridge and he got mad, you know? Kind of violent about it, and wanted to throw her over the bridge! He just went from great, sweet, romantic, lovable to somebody else, even in 11th grade.

GAIL HIGGINS: We used to go to the Fillmore East every week. That's how Johnny and my cousin Janis met, eyes across the room. The Fillmore East was where all the music was happening. Allan Arkush—who did the Ramones' film—was the ticket guy, and he gave us front row tickets for every single show. So that's what we did, that's what we did all the time—just go see music. We would drive in from Long Island. Johnny was living in

Queens, so we would drive in from Long Island into the city, drive Johnny back, drive back to Long Island. That was the ritual.

NINA ANTONIA: Sylvain and Billy [Murcia] went to the same school, which was New Town High in Queens. They kept catching glimpses of Johnny out the corner of their eye, and of course he looked cool. He had long black hair before anybody else, and they were rock 'n' roll kids, too. So what do you do? You gravitate to other people on the same wavelength. They started jamming in Billy Murcia's mum's basement.

SYLVAIN SYLVAIN: We were at Nobody's and I walk up to Johnny and said to him: "Hey! You wanna join our band? Me and Billy have got a group called The Pox. He said: "No, no man. I don't know how to play too good." I said to him, "Don't worry, man. I'll show you how to play."

GAIL HIGGINS: He was the shy boy from Queens and he didn't take drugs. He just had a fabulous look, fabulous sense of humor. When we eventually moved into the city together, he still wasn't taking drugs. There was a big piano in the apartment, and we needed to get the piano out; we had to break it up to remove it. Anyway, in the bottom of the piano there was a big bag of pot. We were all like, "Oh my god, pot, pot! Get it out of the house!" You know, like, "What are we gonna do with this?" We gave it to our friend's sister to sell for us and we split the money, but it was to that extent—you know, like: "Oh my god, get the drugs out of the house!" That's when he started to try and learn to play bass. I used to yell from the other room, "Give up, Johnny!"—'cause I had to hear it over and over and over.

Johnny's first recording was "Dirty Dusty Dungarees," and he and I sang it in one of those pay booths in Coney Island. We sang "Dirty Dusty Dungarees" and "Duke of Earl." But I can't find it.

PHYLLIS STEIN: Must have been around late 1968, '69 when I noticed Johnny at the Fillmore East. I was going there a lot to see blues bands and some British bands and I would see him there with his girlfriend Janis. They stuck out from the crowd. And then I started to go to Nobody's and Max's, and every Sunday, people got together in Central Park. I'd always see Johnny and Syl hanging out, and Rick Rivets and Arthur. That's where I first met them all, with the exception of Jerry. People would hang out at

Nobody's until late. They'd go home, change their clothes, and by noon be at the Bethesda Fountain, walking around, checking each other out. It was a scene.

GAIL HIGGINS: We would drive for eight hours to go see the MC5 or to go see The Stooges. We would go see bands every week. That was Johnny's life, that's what he wanted. You know, when he met Keith Richards he held on to his cigarette packet for months, 'cause he was so excited that he had met Keith Richards! He started out as a fan, and then it turned around where people were fans of his.

BP FALLON: Johnny looked up to Keith Richards, he looked up to Jimmy Page, he talked very enthusiastically of seeing Tyrannosaurus Rex the first time he went to England, which was before he was in the New York Dolls. He went over to England and he had a press pass from a New York magazine and scammed his way into gigs a go-go. Saw Tyrannosaurus Rex and went back to New York and said, "I really, really, *really* have to be in a band."

WALTER LURE: For years before I knew Johnny, through the late 1960s when I was in school, I'd go to concerts at the Fillmore and in the summers to festivals, and I would always see him. Every show that I went to, he was at; it was rare that he wouldn't be there. Probably 'cause I saw some Grateful Dead by mistake, or something like that. He stood out because he had these English clothes on, these expensive British clothes. He was into the same bands that I was, all the British bands and the good blues bands. And Johnny was always there, and he was usually with his girlfriend, Janis. I saw him at Woodstock. I saw him at Atlantic City, at Newport…. He probably thought I was a ghost, following him around.

GAIL HIGGINS: Johnny was the only person who complained about Woodstock, that it wasn't all about peace and love, because somebody stole his fucking leather jacket! And that's all he ever talked about as far as Woodstock went.

MARTY THAU: How I met him was kind of interesting; it was almost like destiny at play: I'm the head of A&R at Paramount. The end of the work day, I am on my way home. I was driving—I had an old vintage Rolls-Royce at that time. And I pull up at a light, and there's this kid hitchhiking in Manhattan. Which I thought was so unusual, so rare. You know, hitchhiking is out in Long Island somewhere, when you wanna go from one town to another.

So I look at this kid and I say, *Hmm, this kid's got to be a rock 'n' roller.* You could just tell by the way he looked, and plus he's carrying a guitar case. So I said, "Okay, come on. I'll give you a lift." So, in this short ride, you know, wherever we were going, he's telling me that he's a potential rock star. He's going to have a great rock band. He's on his way towards stardom and whatever, yet he's hitchhiking in Manhattan. So I said, "Okay, well I'm in music at Paramount. Send me a demo someday— you know, when you get to it. I'd be happy to listen to it, and if I could help you in any way…if I like it, I will." He said, "Oh, thank you very much." I drop him off.

Marcia Resnick: I was teaching in college at the time, so I was not a likely person to be a friend of his. He knew mostly music people, people who hung out, etc., and I met him at the Gramercy Park Hotel. Joy Rider and Avis Davis brought me over there, and I took pictures of him in the bathtub. And this first meeting was very haunting, because I couldn't forget this guy. A couple of months later, he came back from Europe and we became fast friends. He was so intuitively brilliant. He had such a sense of style. I would put all my photographs out on the floor of my loft and he would look at them for a moment and then go, "That, that, that and that." He just knew which the best ones were! I studied photography my whole life and studied art, and I couldn't make decisions like that. He was able to, because of his intuitive genius. And he was that way about dressing and about what clothes to steal for me. He knew the best fabrics and the best designs. He was an aesthetic genius. I have to say that again.

Dolls

GAIL HIGGINS: I remember the night we met Arthur Kane. Johnny and I were tripping and we went to the San Gennaro Feast. It was a very strong trip. We were holding each other's hands so we didn't get lost in this huge crowd, and then we went to Nobody's, which was the big rock 'n' roll hangout. And there was Arthur Kane, this huge figure in the crowd. I remember Johnny and I saying to each other, "They just sent him here because we're tripping! They just sent him here because we're tripping!" And that's how they met.

SYLVAIN SYLVAIN: Arthur Kane, we met him also at Nobody's. And then he came there with this big, tall guy.

RICK RIVETS: Mostly we'd go over to Johnny's, wherever he was living at the time, and he'd show us the songs that he'd come up with on acoustic guitars. Billy and Arthur had met this other Colombian guy.

SYLVAIN SYLVAIN: His name was Rodrigo Salomon. He said, "Man, you guys need a lead singer, and there's a guy in my building that plays the harmonica. He's got long blonde hair and he's a real cool guy, you know?" And that's David Johansen.

NINA ANTONIA: They do their first gig at the close of Christmas 1971, after David Johansen joins the band.

SYLVAIN SYLVAIN: I would fly to England—I went there for the summer—

[then] come back to New York. And now they're playing with David and calling themselves the Dolls. Not the New York Dolls, but The Dolls.

RICK RIVETS: He'd just got back from England, and when he found out that Johnny and Billy had a band together, well, naturally he wanted in.

PETER JORDAN: When I first met the Dolls, John was playing guitar. Before David joined, Arthur had been playing guitar and Johnny was playing bass. As time went by, we learned that Syl's cousin was in a band called The Vagrants. Now The Vagrants were *huge* in New York and opened for basically every band at the Fillmore East. They featured Leslie West, aka Leslie Weinstein, on lead guitar. And Johnny, like I say, in the Dolls at first, he was playing bass.

Well, prior to this, he had a band called The Reign, and Johnny played a Telecaster, just like Leslie West. Apparently they signed a contract with a shyster lawyer in Queens…I shouldn't call him a shyster, he was probably a typical businessman of that era. They cut one song as The Reign, which promptly disappeared—which Johnny never really brought up in his lifetime. Not to me; I'm sure that his girlfriend knew. Syl probably knew. But they made a record. One song of Johnny playing lead guitar in a slightly different manner, but *loud*. Loud was the key. Johnny and loud go together. The only reason I even brought it up is because it ties in a little later.

So any rate, I meet them all (the Dolls) and I'm saying, "Shit, you know, you fucking sound great. You're a great band, you know? The kind of band I've been waiting to hear all my life, and unfortunately I'm not in it. But I'm not doing anything else right now. In fact, I'm fucking sleeping on a floor in somebody's house, so let me start to do a little work with you."

So we started tidying up the amps they rented. Johnny lived with Janis and Billy down on Chrystie Street, right next to, like, a Chinese noodle factory in Chinatown. We started hanging out, and Johnny was an easy guy to get to know. He's friendly, he was affable. He was outgoing. He was very positive. Anything that you played for him that was new with a hot guitar solo and he'd be like, "Holy shit, this is great! I love it I love it I love it!" He was a real ball of energy.

At that point he was definitely not doing any form of opiates whatsoever. All of us—and I mean *all* of us—we all smoked pot, you know? Johnny and Syl, etc. were not into psychedelic drugs very much at all. Have they ever taken them? Of course they took them. Everybody took them in that era. But Johnny was not into that. He didn't smoke. He didn't drink…I mean, he'd have *a* drink. He was the kind if he had a drink, he'd get drunk. And then if he got drunk, he'd probably get into an argument, you know? So it was like, he didn't drink and he didn't smoke cigarettes, and I don't think Janis did either. Syl didn't smoke. David smoked. Arthur smoked. I smoked. David, Arthur and I all drank. Billy was kind of like, catch-as-catch-can. He was a happy-go-lucky type of dude. In other words, if you gave something to Billy, he'd take it—as opposed to Johnny. Syl's much more conservative. David and I were too, cause we'd been around various things which made us wary of too many people glad-handing you. But Billy was a real nice guy. He was like, "Let's party." You know, if there's a party on, I'm going to go to it. And if we're going to party, what is it? You got it? I'll take it. I took it! *We'll party.* A lot of times it worked out, sometimes it didn't—but that's way down the line.

So I met Johnny first just through talking about amplifiers, guitars and other things, and the shows got more and more progressive. He had a really nice guitar—a Dan Armstrong plexiglass guitar—and managed to fuck it up pretty good. There's some old pictures of him with it, and it was nice. He decided to cover it with glue and candy pebbles. Now it looked pretty cool, and it wouldn't have been so bad if they hadn't been *candy* pebbles. Had they been glass or had they been plastic, they would have endured. But the fact that they were candy…. After about the first two shows, they had melted and were stuck permanently in this fucking glue he used and it looked like shit. The guitar is still good. But it looked like shit.

SYLVAIN SYLVAIN: When me and Billy introduced him to marijuana, he said, "Well, okay." You know, [he] smokes a joint. The *next day* he's got a whole pound of pot. He was in excess of everything, that's the whole deal with Johnny.

A big part of the New York Dolls was all the movies that we loved and that were influences on our songwriting. One of Johnny's favorite, favorite movies was the Frank Sinatra movie *The Man With The Golden Arm.* To go back, when we got apartments, our moms would give us their old TV sets. Johnny had a portable one in his room, with the antenna and everything. And every morning, there would be a movie. *The Pawnbroker, Jailhouse Rock*…a lot of rock 'n' roll stuff, and a lot of other crap, too. You know, like

"Que Sera Sera," which Johnny borrowed. And there'd be other TV shows like *The Honeymooners*. That's where he got his line, *can't put your arms around a memory*—that's a *Honeymooners* line. And so one day, we saw *The Man With the Golden Arm* together. It held us captive. This is *before* Johnny was a junkie, we saw this. But it touched us all. Him in particular, because later on I saw almost exactly that story.

PETER JORDAN: When I saw the Dolls, it was like five different personalities. It was very raw. They played an Otis Redding song, a Sonny Boy Williamson song, several original songs, a Shangri-Las song…. And I was like, *They're all sharp and loud.* They were instantly recognizable as a band that was really happening. Johnny was an outstanding part of this, because he was the youngest, he was the loudest, and in many ways, the most flamboyant.

Now the Dolls would use anything that would work, that would fly. They did not wear dresses, but they would wear women's blouses. They would not be in drag, but they would possibly wear women's shoes. They would wear Batman shirts, Superman shirts, velvet pants, crocheted shirts, caps, bags, jewelry. When they left that stage, they were still wearing that type of clothing on the street.

The first person I talked to and spent time with was Johansen. He was the frontman. Also, he was the only person who didn't split the rehearsal immediately. Johnny was wearing a polyester plaid women's suit which he had bought on 14th Street. Now at that point, his muse, his wife, his girlfriend and his oldest girlfriend was Janis, and they would dress in the same costumes.

I had aspirations of wanting to be in a band, being a rock star. The way you dressed, the type of guitar you played…things had to be reflected. Was the guitar cool? Were the shoes cool? Did you *sound* cool? Did you sound *good*? My criteria of sounding good was loud, sharp power chords, like the early Who or the Small Faces or The Kinks. The Dolls were doing this in spades.

Now Johnny was not playing all that many leads, necessarily, but really belting out the chords. He had a natural rhythm, but had a terrible sense of scales, in the sense that Johnny's leads always seemed to have a flat note hidden somewhere in them—which is one of the sounds that makes Johnny Thunders distinctive. You hear a lot of people who play pretty. Sylvain is a good example; you don't hear him hit too many bad notes. Johnny always inevitably managed to put a flat note or a sharp note somewhere in anything he played. But he was charismatic. He was marvelous.

LEEE BLACK CHILDERS: Everybody just lived by their wits. Andy Warhol once said to me, "So you're a photographer?" And I said, "Well, I'm not really a photographer. I don't know anything about taking pictures, but I've got a camera, so it's kinda something I can do." He said, "If you are a photographer, say you're a photographer; then you're a photographer." We were in The Factory at the time. He said, "Look across the room." Candy Darling, the great drag queen, was sitting there smoking a cigarette and drinking a gin and tonic. He said, "See her? She says she's a woman! I guess she's a woman. So you're a photographer. So say you're a photographer." That's what *aaaaall* of us did, including the rock stars, including the New York Dolls, including David Bowie, including The Heartbreakers. We all just said, "That's what we are." And so therefore we were. And that's how I was a photographer. That's how the Dolls were a rock group: They said "We're rock *staaaars!*" And they put on makeup and they put on clothes and they didn't know what they were doing, and lo and behold! That's the secret to it, especially in anything to do with the arts, I think. You just gotta plunge in and do it. When you think back, Picasso, Dali, all of those kinds of people, you just have to say, "This is it! This is art!" And then it either is or isn't. And so in the case of the Dolls, it really was. They were so stunning.

We used to laugh at them when they would come in the back room of Max's Kansas City, because we were old guard by then. We were sitting there, we were "Warhol People." So, *as if.* Candy Darling and Ultra Violet and all those *craaaaazy* people set the standard for all what was acceptable craziness. And then Johnny Thunders walked in with his hair just teased and it was…. We had no idea it was his hair, we assumed it was a wig. We used to call him Wig City. "Oh, Wig City walked in." 'Cause he had *aaaaall* this hair. It was *his* hair! We didn't know that they were pushing *our* boundaries. We didn't know that you could do that! Viva and Ultra Violet and people like that were horrified when they saw Johnny Thunders come walking in, and David Johansen in his silk woman's blouse and his fingernails all painted black…. 'Cause that was *beyond* what they had set as really weird and cool. You couldn't over-shock, and that's what the Dolls did.

LENNY KAYE: I think that all of downtown Manhattan was very compressed. There was a sense that the avant theatre community was bleeding into the avant music community that was bleeding into the avant film community. All of these people gathered in the back room of Max's Kansas City. Certainly there was a sense of Warholian pushing of the boundaries…[a] sense of outrage, and a sense of anything is sexually possible. Anything is…conceptually glittered.

This was a time when, coming out of the hippie era, you would have people suddenly sparkling in a way that they hadn't before. I mean, this wasn't unique to the Dolls. Over in San Francisco, The Cockettes were blurring certain gender boundaries, and the Dolls took that and they played with it. They were certainly guys. It's hard to think of a band that was more male, in a certain way. And yet because of that sense of male identity, seeing them dressed all flashy and garbed in you know, satins and silks…it gave them a sense of *newness*. A sense of starting over.

And it also generated a scene within Manhattan. All of a sudden you had five or six or seven bands playing a certain circuit, from the Club 82 (which was a drag bar), moving out into the boroughs. You had the Harlots of 42nd Street, street punk, the early performances of Kiss. You had a sense of scene growing that would form a foundation for a very elemental sense of New York rock 'n' roll.

ANDY SHERNOFF: I would say they were celebrating Warhol debauchery in their shows. They were coming across as cross-dressers. I mean, they weren't homosexual, but if you didn't know, you'd think, "Oh, who are these fags getting dressed in girls' clothing, playing rock 'n' roll? This ain't real rock 'n' roll." They were playing with gender distinctions, and girls loved it. Girls loved guys dressing up in girls' clothing and putting on make-up.

MARCIA RESNICK: I was intrigued by the way they dressed. We actually all wore shoes from the same shoe store—Tree Mark, an old-lady shoe store—where they could find size-10 women's shoes. I bought shoes there, too. I was particularly intrigued by the way they seemed to be influenced by The Cockettes, a performance group. The Cockettes came to New York and were walking up and down Second Avenue, I remember, and the Dolls were *also* walking up and down Second Avenue, and they all looked the same. They were dressed the same.

Mercer Arts Center

PETER JORDAN: It took a long time for things to happen. 1971–72, we played in New York and stuck at The Mercer Arts Center for a while.

SYLVAIN SYLVAIN: The rent parties sort of paid the rent. We were working in the Oscar Wilde Room of The Mercer Arts Center for almost a year, but that didn't pay all that much.

LENNY KAYE: The first time I became aware of Johnny as a musician was maybe the end of 1971. I was working as a record clerk at Village Oldies on Bleecker Street, and I saw a sign on the wall that said, THE NEW YORK DOLLS AT THE MERCER STREET ARTS CENTER. I love local bands, and though it's hard to believe, at that time there was no local band scene. Because you live in New York, everybody comes through New York, and none of the local clubs really had anything more than cover bands playing for dancers.

When I went to see the Dolls for the first time, I recognized Johnny. Not that I knew him, but down the street from Village Oldies was a bar called Nobody's. Kids who appreciated the English style in rock 'n' roll, that's where they would hang out. I didn't hang out there; I was a little more Bohemian. But I always appreciated walking past there at 2 o'clock on a Saturday morning after I got off work and seeing the girls and the guys doing their mating dance inside. I recognized Johnny as one of the people who I'd see congregating down at Nobody's. So it was great when I actually saw him make the transition from looking like a star to *being* a star, on the stage.

WALTER LURE: So finally, I saw the Dolls for the first time. I went with a few friends and said, "Holy shit, there's that guy I've been seeing for the last 5 or 6 years, and he's in the band." The Dolls were the coolest thing to happen in New York. I still didn't know Johnny. I was just another guy in the audience.

NITE BOB: When I first started to go see them, they were at their first stage of development. I knew there was something happening, 'cause I'd bring friends to see them, and they'd hate them. Anybody who could elicit that kind of negative reaction from my friends had something going for them. It's only half about the music; the other half is about putting it over, and they could put it over! The music was almost secondary sometimes. It was just a lot of energy, they were just a rip-roaring, crazy band. I think that enticed a lot of people. There are a lot of "pro" bands acting really "*pro,*" and the Dolls were very far away from being "*pro.*" They were always late. They were always out of tune. It was chaos. The perfect Dolls gig was a balance between chaos and order. I value my time with them, I really do. I learned a lot. It changed my life in some ways. In a musical way. There was something there—blistering energy.

ANDY SHERNOFF: Word was, there's this great band called the Dolls. I went down to The Mercer Arts Center. It was very exciting. I thought at the time that they weren't good musicians, but now I see old videos and I think they were great musicians. Johnny was a great guitar player. He had a lot of style and knew his rock 'n' roll history.

GAIL HIGGINS: The Mercer Arts Center was a happening place, especially when they were playing. They had a lot of publicity. They had people from all walks of life: They had the art crowd, the rock 'n' roll crowd, the uptown crowd, the downtown crowd, they had the rich people…. Maybe it was curiosity, maybe it was love. I think it was a mixture of all of the above. It was their energy, their look…the fact that people wanted to call them cross-dressers, which they weren't. It was just part of their style, and it was about a time in the city when people were looking for something exciting.

NITE BOB: He was outrageous! The heart of real performance is people want to *be* like the person on stage because they can't be like that. Or they *wish* they could be like that, this outrageous personality with big hair or outrageous clothes or his whiny singing and his brutal guitar playing. There was something in that you could attain. You couldn't be John Lennon, but maybe you could be Johnny Thunders. He was accessible.

If you look at it now, there's hundreds of Johnny clones, in the look or the style [of] guitar playing. He was an innovator. He took a rock look and exaggerated it in 1972. He took Keith Richards and cartooned it, made it bigger and wilder. The clothes were flashier, the hair was bigger, the guitar was louder. He put his whole being into it when he played. Especially in the Dolls.

DONNA DESTRI: When I first saw them at The Mercer Arts Center, it was him and David Johansen that I homed in on. I was a huge Rolling Stones fan at the time. I was a kid, and I saw these guys in their high-heeled shoes and their skin-tight lamé pants and the way they pranced around the stage…I'd seen nothing like it before. They had such charisma, and Johnny was gorgeous in those days, stunningly beautiful. When I saw the New York Dolls at The Mercer Arts Center, it was life changing for me. Like I said, I was a Rolling Stones fan. I was a rock 'n' roll kid, and they were something completely different.

PETER JORDAN: What attracted me most to the Dolls was the *two* guitars. Johnny Thunders was the lead guitarist. Between him and Syl, this became an issue only in terms of who was going to be louder. But they worked really well together, and the fact was, everyone knew how to take the piss out of each other. Other than David, it wasn't five strangers. They had grown up together. They could laugh about it. They were both good guitar players and they were willing to work together at that time, which is very important. There became points when Johnny would play so loud that we didn't have to mic him. We'd mic everybody else in the band, and just let him rip. He was a hell of a solid guitar player and he was a great riff master, but he was not a great soloist. He had a unique style.

RICHARD LLOYD: Having seen them a bunch of times, I thought to myself, *Johnny is not a very proficient lead player*. He had a couple of standardized licks. One of which was a big gliss—if you know what a glissando is, a big *wooooo*. And then Chuck Berry-style, Keith Richards-style, rhythm and leads that were mostly bent pentatonics. It was a limited vocabulary, but he did it superbly. I listened to the first Dolls record again [after] a number of years, and it blew my mind how good they were. They emphasized the glam side without being glam.

Walter Lure: He loved Keith Richards, Eric Clapton, and Jeff Beck, but I don't think he ever tried to play like them, 'cause it didn't come out sounding anything like 'em. He just sort of picked it up. He didn't sound like any other guitar player that I ever knew. I mean, he wasn't like Beck and Clapton and Page and my favorite, McTell; they were great technicians. They could do a lotta stuff and they had phrasing; it was very professional. Whereas Johnny and myself were sloppy. We learned, but we didn't spend zillions of hours over and over so…. I would pick things up from these guitar players. Johnny, I don't know where he picked stuff up, and I never really heard much about what his influences were. He would say, like, he liked this guy, he liked that guy but I never saw the influence in his playing, so it sort of confused me.

John Perry: By the early '70s, when John starts playing those single pickup Les Paul Juniors with that P-90 pickup, you could pick 'em up for $90 in junk shops. They were an unfashionable instrument, and they have a really distinctive sound. You stick that through a twin reverb. You go along the top of the twin and just turn everything up to ten, including the reverb, and you get this unholy noise, which is Thunders. Nobody else turned their reverb up to ten. Then you put a single P-90 into that and bang! It's a very distinctive sound.

Steve Hooker: A Les Paul Junior is one of the best rock 'n' roll guitars that you can get, because it's so simple. It's one pickup, turn on the volume, wraparound bridge, really easy to restring and tune up. He normally played it through a Fender or a Marshall amp. He was quite a loud player. I think he was a better guitar player than people give him credit. He had his chops together. I think he was good.

Dolls loft rent party, 1972
Photos: Marcia Resnick

ANDY SHERNOFF: He knew rock 'n' roll. He had a background in the blues.

LENNY KAYE: The Dolls had a sense of getting back to rock 'n' roll roots at a time when those roots were getting obscured by professionalism and music that was safer. They embodied many rock 'n' roll traditions within them. The blues. The three-chord great hit single. The sense of flash and trash and having a great time. They were wonderful to dance to. I remember many a night they'd be playing, and I'd be out there with girls that I called Miss Ohio or Miss Elvis, 'cause we all had identities. And we'd dance and have a really great, stompin' time. They brought a sense of fun and self-awareness to rock 'n' roll at a time when perhaps things were getting a bit more serious than they needed to be.

FRANK INFANTE: It was like a comic book come to life. You couldn't contrive a better band than that. Looking back now, they're probably one of the best ever rock 'n' roll bands, if not *the* best. Pure rock 'n' roll.

RICHARD LLOYD: As well as being a musician, I think of myself as something of an anthropologist. This New York Dolls show was the first show I had ever seen where the audience was dressed as outlandishly as the band, and they were as interested in each other as they were in what was going on onstage. I thought that Johnny pulled off one of the best reverse Keith Richards that I had ever witnessed. Think of the order of things: Keith Richards had an interest in rhythm and blues. He formed the Rolling Stones with Mick and Brian. They started to tour a lot, so they had to take uppers—you know, drugs—and then they made a ton of money. Okay. And they wrote a lot of original songs, after they were forced to. Well, you get kids in America that do the opposite. They dress up like John, like Keith or Johnny, they do a lot of drugs. They write crappy songs and they go nowhere. Poop, you know? And Johnny's take on that...I mean, the wild hair *up*, the rooster look. And just his general demeanor was very compelling. And quite real in its own way.

The Mighty Thau

MARTY THAU: I had been the head of A&R at Paramount Records, and I resigned because of the petty politics of the company. When I took that position, I thought I could bring a lot of the modern rock. At the time, rock was all the West Coast artists—the Eagles and Joni Mitchell and whatever.... Not that that was my cup of tea, but it was at least rock 'n' roll of a sort. So I resigned.

The night of my last day there, my wife and I went down into Manhattan, to celebrate in a sense. After dinner, we walked around the Village, Washington Square Park...and we happened to stumble upon this marquee: MERCER ARTS CENTER—NEW YORK DOLLS $3. I remembered that someone who I worked with at Paramount—a fellow by the name of Danny Goldberg, who went on eventually to become the President of Warner Brothers, and Atlantic, and Mercury, different labels—I remember him saying to me, "There is one band that I saw that I think are the best unsigned band in New York City, calling themselves the New York Dolls." So we'd seen this Mercer Arts Center marquee, and I looked at my wife and said, "Come on, let's go in. It might be interesting."

The Mercer Arts Center was a complex of six different theaters, and [the Dolls]were appearing in the back room, which was the Oscar Wilde Room. There were 14 people in the audience. I remember thinking, "Hmm, not much of a crowd here. But you know, let's see what it's all about."

So of course the Dolls were notorious for appearing late. If they were supposed to be onstage at 11:30, they would be on stage at 1:00. It was sometimes that long! So we sat. We waited. They came out, and I saw this group—really very wild looking bunch of guys, but I liked their form of rock 'n' roll. Before I went to Paramount, I had worked at a label called Buddah Records and we had lots of bubblegum hits: "Simon Says," "Yummy Yummy Yummy"… they were all gold records. In fact, I think I have 14 gold records from that time. So I understood the construction of [the Dolls'] songs. When you think about it, "Looking for a Kiss"—that's a bubblegum song. I liked it, you know. Different strokes for different folks. There's all levels of appreciation for all different types of audiences.

So at the end of the show, I said to Betty, "I think we've seen either the worst group ever, or the best. Let's go back and talk to them." I'm just curious at this point.

Now around that time of my resignation at Paramount, it seems that this gentleman by the name of Morris Levy, who was the owner of Roulette Records but rumored to be the connection to the Mafia, contacted me. Because I had this great success at Buddah, he said, "I'll finance whatever you want to do, to the tune of $75,000. I said, "I can't do much on $75,000. I would need more than that, but let me think about it." So after seeing this band, the New York Dolls, I thought to myself, "Hmm, there possibly could be some hit singles there. Maybe I should think about signing them and producing some singles." So….

Then I went backstage, started talking to them. They were very humorous. They were always very humorous. After a conversation of about 30 minutes, I thought, "I'd like to know more about these guys." I said, "How about we meet in a couple of weeks in the back room at Max's Kansas City?"—the famous back room at Max's Kansas City, where Andy Warhol and his whole world of people would meet and drink and discuss art. So we did meet, and in the course of this meeting I began to feel that they really had a pretty good idea about who they were and what they wanted to accomplish. And I thought to myself, "I would like to do more than just some singles with these guys. I think I'd like to take them on and manage them." So I dropped that hint, and then in future weeks, maybe a month or two, we met again and I pitched them. I said, "I'd like to manage you. Are you interested?"

At that time, Rod Stewart's manager was also interested in them. It got down to a competition between me and Rod Stewart's manager. They settled on me, because they felt that I had a very strong promotional background—which I did. I concluded that the most important thing for them to succeed would be to get out there on the road. They would have to do a lot of cross-country appearances, and then they'd have to go *back* for it to sink in.

I knew these fellas from my stay at Paramount; big-time booking agents at the William Morris Agency, Steve Leber and David Krebs. At Paramount they said to me, "If there's anything that we can do together, let's do it." And I thought, "Hmm, that's a nice invitation." I approached them and I said, "There's a group that I've seen that I'm taking on in management called the New York Dolls. They're great and they have to get out on the road, and that's your forté. So how about we become partners in management?" They came down and saw them in the Oscar Wilde Room, and we became partners. We signed them sometime in June, 1972. We started devising a strategy. I said, "Let's set up a residency at the MAC, and every Tuesday they'll appear there and let's see how that goes over." It went over very well. Every week, more and more people started coming and before you know it, this buzz went out to the artistic intelligentsia and the social activists. Susan Sontag, David Bowie, Elton John…all these people started showing up, and the buzz was strong.

PETER JORDAN: We had three different managers, which boiled down to a team of two and one. Mr. Marty Thau was the person primarily who was most involved with the band. He had no money, really.

He approached two other people we knew who had money, Leber and Krebs. They all were from management backgrounds. Marty had had many different jobs in his career. He had been a disc jockey—"The Mighty Thau." He had been involved with Tony Orlando, various other types of Brill Building things. Leber and Krebs were two lawyers from the William Morris Agency.

MARTY THAU: I took them into Blue Rock Studios just to see how they would fare in the studio, and to determine how much they knew about recording. In the course of the night, I think we recorded ten or twelve songs, one after another. I didn't bother to do additional takes on each song. I just wanted to see what it sounded like. When I heard it later on, I thought, "Gee, look how slow this is, versus the speed and energy that they put in later versions of those same songs." But it was a good experience for them, and it was good knowledge and information for me.

NINA ANTONIA: Once Marty brought in Steve Leber and David Krebs....
They were from the William Morris Agency. They were big guns to have
on your side. It was like, "Wow! We're gonna be somebody."

MARTY THAU: Some time later after signing them, I'm in a loft on Chrystie
Street. Johnny was living there with Janis. They're sitting over there and
I'm over here, standing. I say, "Okay. Let me give you the rules of this game
we're in which you are about to embark upon. You don't do this, you don't
do that…" Johnny says, "Do you remember me?" I said, "No." He says, "I
was the kid that you picked up hitchhiking in Manhattan." I said, "Well
maybe we were destined to meet later on, and here we are." That was kind
of…what an amazing coincidence.

What were the rules of the game?

MARTY THAU: Don't burn your bridges. Don't do drugs. Don't drink too
much. Be respectful of those who are financing you—you know, your
label. Try to behave yourself, because people that are investing in you want
to feel that you are on board with the game of promotion and marketing,
and you're not a bunch of crazy fools—which they were. They didn't respect the rules at all. Rules for them were made to be broken.

Quaaludes and Red Wine

LEEE BLACK CHILDERS: I was working for *Melody Maker*, and Roy Hollingsworth, who was *the* journalist, said, "Let's go photograph the Dolls." I said, "Ah ah ah, wait a minute, I do Elton John and Rod Stewart and the Stones. What are you talking about?" He said, "No, no. Let's go take photographs of them." So we went down to their loft on the Bowery. I took them into their closet—which wasn't a closet, it was just old remnants of clothes they'd found in garbage hanging from strings all around them—and I took their picture in that… meaning for it to look outrageous. And it caught on in England. It *reeeeally* caught on in England. They looked at 'em and they loved 'em. And then—not to give myself too much credit, 'cause it took me that long—I suddenly thought, "Oh wait a minute. Oh yeah, they're pretty cool. They're all right."

What it comes down to it, with the Dolls—[as] with David Bowie, with so many people who start out their careers with a shock—the Dolls got your attention, then lo and behold, there was something to listen to, and something to pay attention to. And that's what they had. And they could back it up. But they used the women's attire, the makeup, the androgyny and everything. That was just what everyone was doing. We were all dressing out of garbage cans. They were doing it on stage! You know, and sure enough their music was good and then we get to Johnny Thunders and that sound you keep asking me to describe.

We're there in the audience. Darling, we're on acid, we're on speed, we're on cocaine, we're on *anything*, but mostly on poppers. We're crazy, we didn't really care. And then Johnny hit those guitar chords, and suddenly something was hitting right inside our bodies. Suddenly there was *reeeeeal* rock 'n' roll happening. I remember people like, really, really.... Not to put 'em down but, people like Geri Miller and Holly Woodlawn who were just there for the drugs and the craziness, suddenly going, *"Aaaah! What is this?"* and stopping and paying attention. Johnny's guitar stopped you! Even if you were stoned, even if you were *flyyyyyying* high.

The Dolls became a sensation. No one knew what to do with them, least of all the people that ended up working with them.

PETER JORDAN: Everything's going good. We go to Long Island. We do a gig. We go to Jersey, we do a gig. We went out to play a club called Mister D's—which was the title of a Rolling Stones song—a mafia bar, out in Great Neck. Which is where we met Tony Machine. He did a lot for Johnny as well, he worked in the management company. He had been in a band called The Rich Kids. The Rascals were the top. The Vagrants were the second. The Rich Kids were the third. So they send us out to this club. We got there, there's five guys, all with pageboy haircuts and mustaches and so forth, and I think they're covering Deep Purple. They put us in this fucking room. We play for a crowd and Tony is our road manager, 'cause he's supposed to know all these clowns out there. And Billy Murcia steals a bottle from the back bar, and he gets caught. They beat the shit out of Tony. I mean, beat him pretty fucking heavy. Meanwhile, I'm going, "I'm just moving the amps, fellas." And David and Billy get in a huge fucking fight in the parking lot: "You're ruining our career. You're an asshole. You did this. Fucking Tony. Fucking got a split lip." That was the first rift of any kind. So on we go. We're supposed to go to England. Boom-oh! Everything is good. We leave New York on a high note. We play. All the shows are going good. They keep getting better. They get bigger. Everyone knows that they played at Wembley, opening for the Faces, la de da.

MARTY THAU: After a period of them getting strong and more adept at what they did I started talking to record companies but there was this rumor that they were transvestites and gay and crazy and drug addicts...I mean, you name it. The only thing they weren't called at that time—but did get called later on—were communists. Gay communists. Which was so unusual. Record companies steered clear; they didn't want to know. So Steve Leber and I concluded that we should take them to Europe. The audiences and the people are more sophisticated. They will be able to understand who these guys are, where they're coming from, and see them clearly for who they are. Steve had this connection and he got them to be the opening act for Rod Stewart at Wembley. Which was amazing, in that they never appeared in front of more than 300 people, and all of a sudden they are appearing in front of 13,000 people.

We didn't really have the equipment that would project them in such a large auditorium, so people up front loved them and heard every note clearly and all the dynamics…but the back really didn't know. The reviews were kind of mixed. Comments like "This is the future of rock 'n' roll" well before that was stated about Bruce Springsteen…. "They make Slade look soft. These guys are the real deal." That was some of the press that appeared. Some of the other press was, "These guys suck. They can't play for shit… Forget about the New York Dolls."

Sylvain Sylvain: We went on the road with Kevin Ayers and we opened up for Rod Stewart. The Pink Fairies were also on the bill at Wembley Pool, my favorite band of all time.

Marty Thau: One night I'm in my room; Betty had come across to England as well to join me. I'm in my room, and I get a phone call from Billy Murcia, the drummer. And he said, "Marty, you know, I somehow connected with somebody and had a phone conversation and she invited me to a party, and I could use like £5 if you could spare it." And I said, "Sure, no problem, come on down and pick it up." We were in the same hotel. Then when he got there, I said, "Here's the £5, and also our limo is downstairs in front, you could use that. Just tell him to be back here in an hour." Because that night Steve and I were meeting at the flat of Tony Secunda, to meet with Kit Lambert and Chris Stamp, The Who's managers. They had a label called Track Records and they were very interested. In fact, they were at Wembley, and they came backstage.

Kit Lambert was this flamboyant character. When he came into a room, it just lit up. That's how alive he was. Chris Stamp, his partner, was the brother of Terence Stamp, the noted actor. He was very quiet, never said a word. Anyway, we were meeting with Lambert and Stamp at Secunda's to discuss this possible deal. Later in that same week we were going to meet with Phonogram. And there was some other labels in between,

I remember I got contacted by Richard Branson, who invited Steve and I out to his houseboat on the Thames to discuss going with his newly opened Virgin label. That meeting took about six minutes. He said, "We would like to sign you to Virgin and we'll give you an advance of $5,000." I said, "You're a little bit off the mark in terms of the advance—to the tune of about $95,000. We'd like to get $100,000." There were rumors, by the way, that we were asking for $250,000, which was not true at all. $100,000 was enough, and that would have been negotiable. Doesn't hurt to start at the top and work your way down. We said, "Thank you for your interest, Mr. Branson,"—he was 22 at the time—"and good luck with your label."

Back to Billy Murcia. He gets the £5. He gets driven over to this party with people he was meeting for the first time. I'm at the flat with Steve Leber at Tony Secunda's and we're talking when a phone call comes in for me. I'm wondering, *Who has this number and knows that I'm even here?* It was someone—I forgot who it was: "Marty, come quickly. Billy Murcia is dead." What?? I was stunned. I was so stunned and shaken, I just ran out and hailed a taxicab and went to the address that I was given and was led upstairs to the apartment.

It seems that nobody really knew what had happened to him. They put him in a bathtub and tried to pour hot coffee down his throat, and he choked on his own regurgitation and died. Everybody at the party just panicked and ran out and left. They didn't give a damn. They just left this… *kid* who, probably had he not been fed this hot coffee, could have survived. Could have slept it off. They certainly should have called an ambulance, a doctor. But they weren't thinking too clearly. They were more concerned with their own hides and not getting into any trouble. There was probably drugs there that night. Actually, when the coroner's report came in at a later date, he had taken morphine and Mandrax—I guess the equivalent of Quaaludes and alcohol. The coroner's report reported morphine and Mandrax, the equivalent of Quaaludes and alcohol and probably some marijuana. Billy would ingest whatever was available in any amount that he could throw down his throat. He was wild. He was very talented, very creative, and he had an interesting drumming style—but he was living life to the max.

I get there, and the police are already there. I'm led up to this room, and he's on the floor, propped up against a bed. It was heartbreaking. I identified him and then I went downstairs. And the Dolls had already heard about this, and they were downstairs. They were huddled together, crying.

They were really shook up. Tony Secunda, Kit Lambert, Chris Stamp got there, everyone that was connected was there. The first thing I thought: I must get back to the hotel with everyone and call our travel agent and have them book flights out of London back to New York as quickly as possible. I didn't want them to be at the mercy of the scandalous rock press, who would have seized upon that for weeks. I wanted to spare the Dolls and I wanted to spare the Murcia family from all of the bullshit.

PETER JORDAN: Johnny, at this point, is a happy-go-lucky fucking kid, and everything's coming true. Then Billy dies. From misadventure. There's nothing I can say about that. The facts are pretty much there. He went out, he did something stupid. Wrong place, wrong time. His own fault. Other people may be to blame, but essentially it's [his] own fault. He died. *Boom.* That's it.

SYLVAIN SYLVAIN: I remember Johnny calling me up in the hotel—The White House. It's still there today, in London. He said, "Man, something happened with Billy. I just got a call, I'll meet you downstairs." We took cabs over. And I came in the second cab. Johnny had already gone upstairs to the apartment. He said to me, "Sylvain, don't go see him. Don't. He's gone already." And man, that was it. We were devastated. This is when we were being sought out by…we got passed by Mick Jagger, you know, who came to scout the New York Dolls. Johnny took that really personal. A lot of times we were great, and we were still learning our craft, so we were shitty, too—but in a genius kind of shitty way…if I can put it that way.

But what happened was, they put us on the plane the next day. I think Scotland Yard wanted to talk to us and see what happened. They put us on the plane. We were all crying, and the stewardess came up to me and she said, "Why are you guys crying and sad?" and I said, "Yesterday, we were five; today, we're four." It was terrible. Billy's sister, Heidi…you could hear her screams from across the ocean. It was really screwed up.

GAIL HIGGINS: I just remember when they came back and how upset everyone was. 'Cause you know, Johnny loved Billy. They were really, really close. They were all devastated.

Jerry

MARTY THAU: [We] come back to New York after this terrible situation. I'm laid up in bed for a month, and I'm getting phone calls from all around the world looking for some little tidbits of inside information about what really happened. So they were in the worldwide rock press. This little group from New York who never appeared in front of more than 350 people had just played in front of 13,000 people, whose drummer OD'd, so… Took me a month.

I was thinking to myself, "Oh my god, I hope this doesn't end like this." This was my ideal dream band. The Stones and The Who, two of my favorite bands, wanted to sign them to Rolling Stones Records and Track Records [respectively]. We got them on a bill in London opening for Status Quo, and Jagger came down; he was on his way to Southern Italy to his retreat. He saw them. I think he had a mixed opinion about them. [But] he came down.

The Dolls are back in New York. I'm in bed, sick, wondering if the band is over and done with, or what. I get a phone call: "Marty, we're going to dedicate this phase of our journey to Billy Murcia, and we've contacted and located and auditioned this fella by the name of Jerry Nolan, who is a really excellent drummer, and we would like him to become the fifth Doll."

LENNY KAYE: When Billy passed away, it was like a shock to the nervous system because, you know, rock 'n' roll…. You play around with images of obliteration and destruction and living on the edge, and then when somebody topples over the edge, that's almost a wake-up call—it's a tragic thing. I know that Billy was there from the beginning, especially with Syl. To lose someone like that would have destroyed another band. Luckily, they found Jerry Nolan, who was a fantastic drummer. I mean, I don't think people understand how important Jerry was to the propulsive sound, and to gathering these kind of ricocheting elements in the Dolls together. I mean, if you look at what the drums did: You have Arthur, who's playing a kind of quasi-bass, and Johnny's just swiping at the guitar; Syl valiantly trying to rhythmically hold it together, and David the showman. So you needed something to anchor it. And when Jerry came aboard, even though it didn't mitigate the sense of tragedy, all of a sudden you felt like the Dolls came into focus musically. And it propelled them into the next step of their artistic development.

SYLVAIN SYLVAIN: Life goes on. A lot of people came up to us and said, "That's it. You should quit. You shouldn't do it anymore. There will never be another Billy. There'll never be anything you can replace him with. Blah blah blah. And you should just quit."

In the 1960s, when me and Billy were in Pox, there's another guy in Queens that used to hang out with us all the time, and he was a musician. Him and his friend, Gregory, the bass player. He was in this band that was called Shaker, with Jerry Nolan. He was the drummer. Now Jerry's older than us. I don't know how many years. And he would always say, "Oh man, I love your band. And you should go play over there. You should go play over here." By the way, one of his girlfriends back then was Bette Midler. Jerry Nolan went out with Bette Midler. We were all kids trying to make it and trying to get heard.

Anyway, we had this open jam session to find a new drummer. We tried like 10 or 20 people. One of them was Mark Bell, and of course, Jerry Nolan. But I knew deep down there was a message that Billy Murcia communicated with me. Before he died, he said, "If anything ever happens to me, Jerry should be the drummer." I don't know *why*. For a spooky reason…it happened. I was the guy who called him up and said, "Jerry, you're the next New York Dolls drummer. Congratulations." And he said, "Yeah man? Oh yeah, babe." You know the way he talked. And he became our drummer.

ANDY SHERNOFF: There's nothing better for publicity than a death in a band. Billy Murcia was a very rudimentary drummer. Jerry Nolan had a little more style. He's a technically a better drummer, and it really helped finesse the sound. Jerry Nolan had a unique style, he had a look, and that made them the band that we think of today.

PETER JORDAN: Now Billy, Johnny and Syl were very tightly bonded. I don't think there was any question of it going to stop. Billy wasn't a songwriter. He was a drummer. He was everybody's best friend. He was the nicest kid you wanna meet, but it was like, what the fuck?

Jerry says that he talked everybody into continuing. Fact was, we auditioned a lot of drummers. It came down to him and Marky Ramone. Jerry had the better personality. I don't know if you know Marky Ramone, he's a great fucking guy, great fucking drummer, but he wasn't the right fit. Jerry had known Billy, and he was from Queens. He was a guy that was always on the scene. In fact, we used to rent drums from him sometimes.

NITE BOB: Jerry was very different than the rest of the Dolls. He came from a different kind of background and upbringing. Why was he the perfect drummer for the Dolls? I think you'd have to talk to the band. I mean, obviously it worked. He did have a '50s feel, and there is this '50s feel to the Dolls, right? Some of these other guys were maybe *too* proficient for what they were doing, because there was a big girl-group influence in the Dolls, more than most people realize. When you are in a band and you're trying somebody out, you know in a couple of minutes if it's working, because there's a feel, a vibe, you know, and then it's like, "Okay—you're the guy. Let's go." And off they go.

WALTER LURE: Jerry was a great drummer. He was a natural, because he never practiced. When I knew him, the guy never picked up a drumstick when he wasn't on stage. He just had this natural ability. He probably learned when he was younger. He had to practice, obviously. He was into Gene Krupa, but he would always get the beat right. The perfect beat.

NINA ANTONIA: Jerry had an interesting history, musically. He'd played with Suzi Quatro. He'd played in Wayne County's band, Queen Elizabeth. He was a really good drummer. A really solid drummer, and he was a little bit wiser and older than the rest of the Dolls as well. So he comes in. He auditions. He gets the job. And he brings them up to speed.

Jerry

PETER JORDAN: The songs came pretty quickly. They were reasonably simple, because of the fact that we weren't playing too far apart. And we had an established base for a while at The Mercer Arts Center and at Max's. We'd rehearsed prior to the shows, so this was the material that was developed for the first LP—which was pretty much all written before we'd even gone to England.

Jerry joined the band, we had to start rehearsing. Now certain things started to happen, one of which was that I would rehearse primarily with Johnny and Jerry, and I would play bass. We did a lot of rehearsals like that, because they were efficient. Johnny and Jerry got along. We were able to book space and we were running over old material and we didn't need a vocalist. The vocals were like the icing on the cake. The songs were simple enough that once the arrangements were there, David could step in and we'd pick them up. Arthur was beginning to develop a little antisocial behavior. He would not be really available in the early hours, and Johnny was someone who always loved to play. He loved jamming. He loved playing. We would play—we'd rehearse for four or five hours, no problem, all the time, so things were starting to come together.

NITE BOB: David was the ringleader at that point and Johnny was his foil, but Syl and David had more of the same musical basis. I think Johnny had that same basis, but he was a bigger personality. Jerry was the outsider. Arthur was Arthur; he was there from the beginning and he was part of that energy and part of what they did. Artie was a lot of fun.

MARTY THAU: David was this androgynous front person. Johnny was the counterpoint to that; he was the butch figure. Although when you spoke to him behind the scenes, he didn't portray himself as this rough and tough, gruff butch figure. He was quiet. He was sincere. He was gentle. Soft spoken, you know? He was a delightful person. *But…*for the public, he was this Mr. Bad Boy.

Arthur was a creative mind. He had some good ideas, but so did Syl. Jerry didn't speak much about things like that. He was the drummer, and was instrumental in giving them good thoughts about how to emphasize certain dynamics. He taught them a lot. Me and Steve set up a dinner for the Dolls. I see this guy and I'm thinking, *He doesn't look the part at all.* I mentioned this to David, and he said, "We will turn him into a Doll. Don't worry about that. Leave that to us."

PETER JORDAN: Now the problem was, again, there was no real interest. We now had management that was pretty cohesive and some money, but the band had to reorganize. So we started rehearsing more frequently. We were still playing the same circuit around the city. The hunt now was on for a record company. The band had tremendous interest and press, which now was running pretty much 50/50 negative and un-negative.

BOB GRUEN: Tony Machine, who worked at the management office, said, "Why don't you come down and see the New York Dolls at The Mercer Arts Center?" They also managed Elephant's Memory, who were associated with the Hells Angels. (The Mercer Arts Center was right off 3rd Street, where the Hells Angels' headquarters were.) So one night, I stopped into The Mercer Arts Center. I remember seeing a lot of strange looking people. Some guy walked by me wearing eye shadow and eyeliner around his eyes, and I was out the door in a second, because I didn't hang around with guys like that. You know, the Hells Angels didn't do things like that! I wasn't really used to that.

Tony said, "You gotta come back again, you gotta see this band, the New York Dolls. They're really great." It was an interesting place. There were a couple of rooms where the bands played, and there was a room in the middle where there was a bar, there was a kitchen.... It used to be the old ballroom for the Broadway Central Hotel, and in the kitchen, there was an experimental video group; they're still called The Kitchen today.

There was another room that had a boutique, they had plastic mini-skirts and platform shoes, the kind of clothes I hadn't really seen before. I noticed a lot of the girls walking around in the mini-skirts...that was much more interesting than the guys in make-up.

I was waiting for the band to come on the stage, and they didn't come on, so I left. And Tony said, "*No*, you gotta come back again, and you gotta see the band." So I came back. The next time, I remember standing around, waiting by the bar in the middle for the band to come on this little stage, and there was no band there or anything. I saw people going in and out of a door on the side somewhere, so I went in through the door, thinking it was the restrooms or something, cause a lot of people seemed to be going in and out. I walked in and all hell broke loose.

Jerry

It was the Oscar Wilde Room, and it was just this big crowd of people. One side had a really steep wall, like bleacher seats; it was just like a wall of people, it was so steep. And in the middle was this big crowd of people, and in the middle of *that* was the band—just jumping around, all crazy-like, wearing make-up and, you know, unusual clothes.

Some people say that the New York Dolls dressed like girls or women, but they didn't look anything like any women…*I* didn't know any women that dressed like that. They might have bought a shirt that was in the ladies department. But nobody wore it the way they did. They were just bright and loud and colorful, and the music was the same. Bright. Loud. Colorful. Chaotic. It didn't look like it was rehearsed. It barely came together. It was like a train wreck in process, everything just tumbling and crashing around…but it was exciting. It was very exciting.

And it was hard to tell which was the band and which was the audience, because people were dancing all over. I figured out that the guys with the instruments must have been the band, and the other people, who were just jumping around, were dancing, and they were the audience. But there were just so many people and so much chaos going on…it was one of the more exciting things I'd ever seen, and I became an instant fan. I remember coming back a couple of weeks later for New Year's Eve and I brought some of Elephant's Memory with me, the drummer and the saxophone player, Rick Frank and Stan Bronstein.

Toby Mamis had been the publicist for the New York Dolls, and he was also the publicist for Elephant's Memory. He said, "I'll set you up a photo session with them." So he told me to come down one afternoon when they were rehearsing, and I met Arthur and I think I met Jerry. Not sure if I met Syl or not, but Johnny and David weren't there yet. Somebody had just gone for a sandwich. I waited around for about an hour and they didn't show, and so I left. But at New Year's, I remember meeting Arthur.

I was standing there with Rick and Stan, and he came walking by, so I introduced them. I said, you know, "This is Arthur." And Arthur said, "Oh, hello boys." You know, he had like a yellow sequined ladies bathing suit on and a see-through cellophane yellow tutu, like a ballerina skirt, and these yellow sparkly tights and engineer boots that he had painted yellow, and I think he had a little pink chiffon kind of scarf or handkerchief tied around his wrist. And he was like, "Hi, guys." And I was like, *Woooah!* And I remember him walking away and Stan Bronstein going, "What the hell was that?" And I said, "The bass player, you're going to love these guys." He said, "I don't know about that." And actually, two years later Stan Bronstein played the saxophone solo on the New York Dolls' "Human Being," one of their better songs. Because they *did* get to be really good friends—once you got to know them! Once you got past the shock of what they looked like, they were all pretty nice guys.

It was interesting to me that the Hells Angels, who were trying to get women and stuff and had these fat biker chicks with them, hanging around there at the clubhouse.... And when I went to see the New York Dolls, they had much more attractive looking women, but they treated them really rough: "Get off my lap. Get away from me! What are you trying to do, honey? Step back. Give me some space here." They weren't coming on to them at all. They were actually pretty macho, and the girls seemed to like that a lot. It seemed to me after getting to know them a little while, the New York Dolls were more macho than the Hells Angels, which was kind of a surprise. I mean, they didn't really *try* to come on to girls the way most guys do, and they weren't being really nice about it. They were just being real and being themselves. They treated them in a very real way, and that impressed me a lot.

Mercury

Marty Thau: On December 19, 1972, they were to appear in the biggest room at The Mercer Arts Center, which held about maybe 300 people and it was like a record convention. All the presidents of different record companies came down and the press was there. It was like a big event. They did two shows. The first show was mixed. They were nervous, and it was really the first show they were playing with Jerry, although he held up his end very capably. But the *second* show that they did, when all the record execs had left, they were great. But…that was that. So that didn't help their cause very much in terms of getting a record deal.

So we said okay, we'll just go further. We'll go as far as we can go. We will book them out into the suburbs and uptown and downtown. We will keep booking them and making it hard to ignore this band, and sooner or later, something should break through. There was one A&R person, Paul Nelson—the brilliant, late Paul Nelson—who spotted them and said, "This group is great. I want to sign them." But every label had a different opinion about why they wouldn't sign the group. They're too gay or they're too this or they don't play enough. David Johansen looks like a star or David Johansen sucks or Johnny Thunders is a wild man or…. Everybody had a different opinion.

Sylvain Sylvain: What happened was, we were not getting signed. We were playing the big theater—not the Oscar Wilde Room—for over 500 people. But that was to our fans and to the kids that were our generation. A big mix; such a groovy bunch. Truman Capote was in our audience. He probably was our biggest fan. Steve Leber comes up with this idea to have a showcase, to showcase the New York Dolls in that big theater to the whole industry. He said after that, we'll get a deal. It didn't work. First of all, we had no fans there. And sometimes Johnny would take a long time to tune up, 'cause don't forget we used—this is before they had tuners—so we tuned up with David's harmonica. So David: "Rrrrrrrrrrrrrr ding ding ding de de de dong dong." "No, that's wrong. Okay, do it again." "Da ding dongdong dong," you know—20 minutes. It seemed like a lifetime. Poor Johnny. He had...sometimes he had a little bit of you know, strange ear. Specially on tuning. But, I mean, we all had our little faults and we were kids learning our craft, but it was beautiful. It was great. So....

Yeah, this is the biggest worst bad move that you can ever do to this band. First of all you take away their fans. We had no more screaming chicks or guys passing around joints. Now you have guys in business suits passing around mirrors of cocaine. This is not good! So we do this show-case. We play terribly, as far as they're concerned. What happened was, we get passed by every company: Columbia, RCA, Warner Brothers. And every other little affiliate, well, they're all part of the big picture. They are not independent like we have today. Even in the late '70s, there was no independent records. You would only get signed if you could sell as many records as The Beatles or The Rolling Stones. This was a brand new thing that was created by the New York Dolls, this brand new music. All they were interested in was selling millions and millions of records. If not, they don't want to even touch you. Who the hell's going to fuck with a band that can't even tune up and be prepared and deliver? Like the way they want it to be delivered. On a golden plate, basically. So we get passed by everybody. Everybody, everybody, *everybody*. The only record company that didn't show up that night was Mercury Records, and one of our fans from there, Paul Nelson.

MARTY THAU: Paul Nelson keeps badgering the president of Mercury Re-cords—that was who he worked for—to sign this group. And Irwin Stein-berg, who was the president at the time, he says, "I don't want any part of this group. They're revolting. This is not someone that we need on our label." He was trying to invent a new golf club. This is who we had to deal with, instead of someone who could see the potential influence of this rock 'n' roll band and this refreshing new look and whole new approach. He refused to allow Nelson to perform his A&R function, which was to sign people that he liked.

Months later, Nelson knew that Steinberg was in New York from Chicago, where he was based. He showed up at his hotel at 6 o'clock in the morning and waited for him to come down. When Steinberg saw this, he said, "If these are the lengths that my A&R guy would go to show up so early to catch my ear again, I'll give him a break. Sign them." So we had a contract at that point. It was a decent contract. There was an advance. It was not $100,000, it was not $50,000, but it was not much less than that and it was a whole new set of equipment that they purchased for them and a guarantee of two albums—which was good, because you figured the first album would just be the breakthrough, to open the door. The second album would, you know, solidify them more.

SYLVAIN SYLVAIN: Paul Nelson is the guy who used to roommate with Bob Dylan when they were in college, and it was Bob Dylan who stole all his records. Paul was like…he had always like a rusty beanie kind of hat, he smoked Sherman cigarettes. He's a real cool guy. Very beatnik kind of looking cat. Thank god he said to Mercury, "You gotta sign these guys, 'cause they're gonna get signed." He didn't realize that everybody had passed on the New York Dolls. Clive Davis, and the presidents of all these companies, you know. The next thing is we get called and we go to this office, I forget exactly where it was. We sign all together and then we took pictures. There's a picture of Paul Nelson, Marty Thau…the Dolls, of course, and the lawyer who put it all together. I think it was a three-album deal. Since the Dolls started in 1970, by 1973 we had songs like "Personality Crisis," "Frankenstein," and "Trash".… Hit records, but never put on vinyl. These were hit songs to our fans. They knew those songs better than we did. They could probably tune up Johnny's guitar, too, better than we did also, but that's besides the point.

PETER JORDAN: None of us were getting any money at that point. After we came back from Europe and Jerry joined, we went on to a salary basis. The band [members] were getting $250 a week, and I was getting $100 a week. That remained my salary from the time I started to the time that I left the Dolls. Plus, whatever perks that you could scratch out of it, such as what they call *per diems* when you're on the road. But I was getting a hundred bucks a week, so I was happy as a pig in shit.

We started to rehearse a little more vigorously, because we needed to become slightly more professional. And we realized ourselves—from playing at slightly larger venues in front of audiences that didn't already know us—that we had to tighten up.

The main thing that happened was, everybody moved from one-room apartments to two-room apartments. The status started to change with Johnny, in that relationships started to fray among your older friends.... Things became more intense. So older friends became more marginal, and we became more and more compartmentalized.

We were now a five- to seven- to eight-piece core group of people who were now working on this with management. We still hadn't even got an album yet. Leber and Krebs were trying to get us out and about so we could play for an audience that was at least was national. We opened for Mott the Hoople, who were pretty well known at the time…they were perceived as being compatible to us. They had come up the long road themselves. They were considered a part of the glam scene, which was pretty ephemeral. Involved everything from thugs putting butterflies on their cheeks to people whose music reflected a kind of more open thing. Bowie was a good example. He had popped up around The Mercer Arts Center, but he gave the band some credibility. There were mainly bands that people thought were half shit and half good. You had Alice Cooper, who were a pretty hard goddamn rock band. Stooges were everybody's favorite losers, but were tremendous. Mott the Hoople were on a weird cusp, coming out of an English underground.

We had bought new amplifiers. That show was a real eye-opener. It was an outdoor show; middle of the afternoon in front of a pretty big crowd that never heard of the band. Could have gone better, could have gone worse, but we were working away. Jerry hadn't fit all that much in the band, yet. He was a hot drummer. The band was good. They did play faster, quicker—they had been rehearsing more. Johnny was very on the ball. Everyone was energetic at this point, we really had something to prove. The songs were there.

Johnny would smoke pot like Bob Marley. I mean, we all did. Johnny and Syl lived together on 14th Street. I would go over there. We'd sit around. We'd smoke joints. We listened to music and then we'd go rehearse and then we'd go play. Kind of every day went like that. I used to hang out a lot with Arthur. We were compatible. We got a valet-cum-all-round-gofer type of guy. So as the shows got more complex, you would need someone who does not have to worry about the sound or the amplifiers. This was Christian Rodriguez, Frenchie. And he was an integral part of the band. He had been working at various used clothing places in the East Village and he was a tremendous provider of costumes. He was Puerto Rican. He had been a sergeant in the army, believe it or not, and he was a really hand-some, good looking guy. He became kind of the guy who would control the dressing rooms; he was kind of like our pimp, in a manner of speaking. (There's a famous scene of him trimming Syl's armpits in one of Gruen's videos.) We had a little cohesive unit. So we're working away and against all the odds we get signed to probably one of the lower-tier record labels in America, but we get signed.

LENNY KAYE: I think the Dolls were a dangerous signing, because they were kind of hard to control. You didn't really know what was going to happen, whether it was going to be a great show or a scattered show, and as characters, they got out of the comfort zone of a lot of record labels.

Mercury was part of the Phonogram empire. In Europe, they had a very big standing, I had a lot of Mercury records in my collection. Rod Stewart was on there. They were a legitimate major label contender. In the Dolls, Paul Nelson saw what he hoped rock 'n' roll could aspire to. He was not only a musician and a musical person, but he was also a writer, so he could stand back and look at them conceptually and also enjoy them musically. He could see that they were at the beginning of what could have been a long career, because the writing was very sharp and precise. Great hooks, great choruses.

And in some ways, maybe it would have been a case where the audience would have had to catch up to them, rather than following the trail of what was popular at the time. Certainly the Dolls were avatars of a sound that was lodged somewhere later in the '70s, Their attitude of erasing the old and bringing in their own sense of the new. Their presumptuousness. I hate to use the word, but their *punkiness*. They were really like punks, you know? "We know what we're doing, we're going to go for it!" And it made for a really powerful presentation that seemed—especially in the small borough of Manhattan—was definitely going take over the world. But of course, you go across the Hudson into the great underbelly of America and you realize that people are not as sophisticated and as hip as you would like. And maybe they would become so over the next few years. But for the Dolls, they went out there and it was like Davy Crockett going out into the wilderness. They had to prove themselves all over again.

Marty Thau: I started looking around for a producer. Most of the producers felt that this was a troublesome unit; they had no idea. Eventually, Todd Rundgren came into the picture, and he said, "I'll produce them." It's interesting. He was going to produce them and then go down to Florida to meet with Grand Funk Railroad, that was his next production function. And they had that record out of that session, *We're an American Band*, which I think was a number one record. He comes in.

There were mixed opinions in the group about him. Jerry Nolan felt that he didn't present the drums as fiercely as they should have been presented. I don't necessarily disagree with that. I think he did a pretty damn good job, as it turned out. That first album's considered a rock 'n' roll classic. The reviews on it were, I would say, 90 percent rave and okay. So we had a good record at that point.

Sylvain Sylvain: Well as production is, it's always like, who's available? It's almost the same way as how we got our record deal. Why do we go to Mercury? Oh 'cause they were the world's best record company? No. It's what happened. We wind up with Todd Rundgren, who gave us a great record. I think it could have been even better. I agree with Jerry Nolan and with Johnny in a way, that the drums don't sound good. End of story. And when you went up to him to talk to him about it, he didn't really want to listen. And he was there with his little dog and his girlfriend, Bebe Buell. We went to the Record Plant by way of a studio in New York on 43rd Street, right off of Broadway. The engineer was Jack Douglas, who became a producer, but at that time he was only the engineer. The little dog that Todd had peed on the control booth, and it was, "Okay, that's going to help the sound for you guys." Thank you. And one night I remember coming in there and he had all the music shut down except for David's overdubs. So David, all by himself, just like going, "bleeeer PERSONALITY Arrrc-cchhgh!" And yeah, you put it alone like that, it's horrible. The best thing that he did was put me on the left-hand side and Johnny Thunders on the right-hand side. Left and right. Stereo. That was genius, and I carry that on, on the second album.

PETER JORDAN: I know that you can't go on forever. But Johnny was very consistent. He was writing songs. He was doing good. He hadn't got into smack. He was a typical kind of wise guy. In this day and age, it's almost quaint. He didn't smoke cigarettes. He really didn't drink. He was smoking a fair amount of pot and he played guitar every day. The record session could have been more professional. It could have been more coherent but…otherwise it wouldn't have happened at all. It seems like it took forever. I think it took two weeks, 16 days, something like that. They made an album.

LENNY KAYE: I liked the choice of Todd Rundgren as producer. Todd was familiar with the New York scene. Todd was familiar with the Dolls' world; he was no stranger to flash and trash himself. And I also know Todd's producing philosophy, which was, "If you know what you want, I'll get it for you. If you don't know what you want, I'll do it for you." I think in retrospect, the New York Dolls' first album captures them about as well as you could capture them. It certainly could have been a little more…*polished*, but this was the Dolls. You wouldn't want that. I think it caught their raw energy, which in a sense, is what a first album should do. Capture what makes a band magic. By the third album, then you can get a little more professional because you've done your growing. But for a first album, I thought Todd did a great job. I'm sure it was hard to maintain control, since from what I understand, the sessions were quite the instant party. But to me, the album always spoke to what the Dolls strengths were, which was a raucous good time.

NITE BOB: Every band complains about their record! You know. I think it was very, very accurate recording of where they were at that point in time. They were always moaning about something, you know, especially Jerry and Johnny…. I don't think anybody could have done a better job.

NINA ANTONIA: You get tracks like "Vietnamese Baby" which is politically aware, you know. You've got the Vietnam War going on and we mustn't forget that. We mustn't forget the times that this was recorded in, and we may sit back now and wonder, well, why were the Dolls radical? But I don't think there were many people that wrote a song as pertinent as "Vietnamese Baby".

SYLVAIN SYLVAIN: Arthur was really a prolific writer, although he only got one song in the New York Dolls, which is "Private World," but it's so like him. Jazzy, almost. It's really cleverly written. Most of the lyrics were done by David, and the music was done individually by whoever came up with whatever...that's how it was. I have to admit, Johnny Thunders and David Johansen took the aggressive, like, "Hey this is me and this is mine and blah...." And they wouldn't give the other guys the same balance. This is very true. Exactly what happened. But for the most part, if you had something good, you know, it would get put on. It would get written and something would happen.

BOB GRUEN: When the New York Dolls' album came out, I mean, they had their fans but they also had a lot of people who hated them, and when the New York Dolls would play a show they would come on a bit late. There was this tension building up and building up like, "When are the Dolls going to come out?!" And finally they would hit the stage, and the audience would jump and start screaming and yelling and they would kind of divide—sort of smashing into each other, actually, with half the people running to the stage, and half the people running to the door to get out. It was really a love it or hate it kind of situation. For a lot of people, it was the best thing they'd ever seen. For a lot of people, it was the worst thing they'd ever seen.

In an actual, legitimate, "the voters vote" kind of vote in *Creem* magazine, they had a reader's poll and the New York Dolls won best new group of the year. They also won *worst* new group of the year. I suggested to Marty Thau that he use one of my pictures for an advertisement. It's the same picture, and it says "Best New Group of the Year. Worst New Group of the Year. New York Dolls. Get the Record and make up your own mind."

They were on *Don Kirshner's Rock Concert* on TV, which was one of the very few places you'd actually see any rock 'n' roll. Don Kirshner always came on and talked about what a wonderful new group this was, but when he put on the New York Dolls, it was almost a disclaimer. He said, "A lot of people are talking about this group, and a lot of people like them and a lot of people don't like them, and we're not sure." Like, instead of backing them up himself, he said, "We're not sure, so we're going to put them on TV and we'll let you, the viewers, decide...." Nobody knew what they were.

NITE BOB: Mercury Records wasn't ready to deal with what they were, you know? I mean they didn't know how to market it. It was a little ahead of its time for mid-America, outside the hot spots of New York, LA, Detroit, Chicago, Cleveland. Middle America are the people who really buy the records. It was a little too extreme for those people. The album cover of the first record really hurt them. They never looked like that. Never. I mean, like, the sense of outrage? Yeah, okay. But it put people off. It was very shocking, very out there. And then when they go to see them, they didn't look like that at all. They were much more—you know, kind of fashionable street look. But that's my opinion, you know. I mean, other people may feel differently. That album cover may have changed their life, for all I know.

MARTY THAU: Mercury hoped that the Dolls would appeal to that blander American audience, but that was not where the Dolls were coming from. That audience, in time, learned what that was all about and tried to, you know, get in with that style. What would you say? The Dolls were out of their time? Yeah. Sure. Definitely.

BOB GRUEN: The record company had not actually seen the band play, and so we had this idea that we were going to make a videotape and send them the video. Now in New York, we were kind of advanced; we were getting used to seeing videos of the band. The record company hadn't seen them, so we made a tape to show them what the band was like.

In their regular, kidding-around way, we made a video in the dressing room at Max's where David introduces the different members of the band: "This is Johnny and Syl…." I remember he introduced Jerry Nolan, saying that he played the world's first instrument, the drums. And so we sent the video out to Mercury Records, to the executives. Now they didn't really just put it on a desk and you know look at it the way we had been doing it, kind of casually. They rented a *screening room*, cause they didn't really know much about filming.

So they were sitting in a rather formal screening room and they saw this rather *in*formal videotape, and they were really shocked. They didn't know what they had on their hands. They didn't know how to sell it. The New York Dolls were kind of androgynous, and they were new at the time, men who were just so *out there*. Nowadays there's a word called metrosexual, which describes men who care about their looks and go to great lengths about grooming and shaving and unusual hair styles and unusual combinations of clothes, people who are really into the way they look—but back then, that was quite unusual.

And nobody's really topped the New York Dolls for the way they looked. They each had style and class, and they just really looked great; but for a lot of people it was very frightening. They see a man who has some makeup on…they would think that they were homosexual. In 1972, 1973, being homosexual was still illegal; it wasn't just looked down upon. So they didn't know how to sell the New York Dolls, because they looked like they were gay.

In my video, Jerry Nolan talks about it. He said a lot of men didn't understand, they didn't know whether they were gay or not gay, but the girls understood. The girls totally knew. There's nothing gay about the New York Dolls in any way. The whole point of dressing up to look like a Doll is because girls like to play with dolls! And the Dolls, the New York Dolls, wanted girls to play with them! So they figured, if you dress up to look like a doll, then the girls are going to like you. And it actually worked.

NINA ANTONIA: Malcolm McLaren. He's over in New York doing a fashion fair in '73, possibly the summer, and because of Sylvain, the Dolls go to this fashion fair and they meet McLaren, play him a copy of the first album. He said to me that he fell about laughing because he just thought it was so bad; that they were so great at being bad. He called them the worst striptease rock 'n' roll band, but he adored them nonetheless and became an avid follower of theirs.

California

SYLVAIN SYLVAIN: Our first album had just come out, and we were scheduled to play Max's Kansas City for 6 nights in a row. We sold it out, two shows a night...it was a small place. What happened was, all our girlfriends supposedly...they were going to go out to California, and Arthur had met this girl who said that she was one of The GTOs, Miss Connie is her name. But she *wasn't* in The GTOs, the girl band; you know, Girls Together Outrageously. She put up this story when she came to New York, I guess, to meet people, but Arthur Kane fell in love with her and they had this romance. After we finished our shows at Max's Kansas City, we had one night off and I get a call from him and he said to me,"I'm in the Hospital at Beth Israel." At the time he was living on top of the bar on First Avenue and like, Second Street. So I call up Johansen and I said, "Hey, Arthur's in the hospital." "What happened?" "I don't know. Let's just go see."

We get together, take a cab up to Beth Israel. Arthur's been stabbed in his thumb. He said that Miss Connie asked him to take her out to Los Angeles, because that's where she's from. She wants to come there with the big band or whatever (to prove) she's made it! And he said, "No no, we don't have any money...." But Cyrinda Foxe, who was going out with David, *was* going. So Connie apparently hacked his thumb or maybe tried to hack him.

It almost got his tendon, which would have really screwed him up. But they bandaged him and put a cast on it so he wouldn't move it and it would heal. Arthur was always a big drinker. Me, I like to smoke a joint and that's the end of that. You know, I drank too. And I still do. I can still enjoy it. But Arthur, he was...he was pretty in there. Like Johansen, too. Johansen was really into it. They would like to drink you under the table as a challenge. That's their school. Not so much me and Johnny, you know? Back then, we had, you know, started to trip on whatever it was; it wasn't LSD...maybe it was. But who knows? It wasn't heroin. It wasn't cocaine. Too expensive. Although we had some friends that were big dealers and they would invite us up. They would supply big bands, and the New York Dolls was the next thing...so they'd help us out by fucking us up.

Anyway, [we had] Peter Jordan, who was always one of our roadies, along with Max Blatt and Desmond. Nite Bob was our sound man, but not for the California trip. So Peter Jordan was also a bass player cause when we were going out to Los Angeles we were also on television, playing live, we did *The Midnight Special*—where you can and cannot see it's Arthur Kane out there playing and he's got a cast on. But there's a guy behind his amp that's really playing—that's Peter Jordan.

MARTY THAU: Steve Leber started booking state by state, city by city. They went out to California. They appeared at the Whisky a Go Go and they sold out four evenings, two shows a night, in three hours; they'd sold out every one of those shows. I mean, for a group that never appeared in LA, that had their first album out, that was a pretty impressive feat. The press showed up, and the fans, the groupies, were there *en masse*. They were very successful shows.

PETER JORDAN: The album came out. Now there was the ability to actually get out of town. And remember, we really never got anywhere but Ohio. I literally cannot remember going anywhere else...maybe like, Buffalo or Long Island or something.

So the record came out and everybody's very positive. Everything is up. And we're going to go to Los Angeles. This is where the videos started to come in. Right around this time, and in this period of time, we had met Gruen and he was a photographer. He was doing some work with Yoko Ono, and through that, they literally bought and gave him and his wife this video equipment. So he started filming us. The first films he did were right before we left for Los Angeles, after the first album was recorded. We played a full week—I think it was five or six days at Max's.

Max's was very small. I don't know if you've ever been there, but it was small. This is before they even opened up the top floor. At one point Max's became a big square room, but in the early days, it had a fucking kitchen in the middle. So it was shaped like a long hallway. And a kitchen of all things, in the middle on the top.

So anyway, it got more and more and more and more and more packed. Everything was going good. The album was finished. It was just being released. I don't think the band could have been, at that point, any more on top of it.

So the fifth night, Arthur goes home. He has a contretemps with his girlfriend at the time and she mutilates his hand. She tries to cut his thumb off. And she does a pretty fucking good job. She really fucks it up. So, that's let's say, Thursday morning.

Thursday afternoon I get a call from Johnny. Johnny, strangely enough, was always the guy who communicated with me. Everybody else was like "La de da…." Johnny called me up. He said, "Can you play the songs?" And I said, "Yeah, I can play them. I've got to rehearse them." So he, Jerry and me go down to Max's and we rehearse for four hours and we play the fucking show. It's the last night of the series. Show goes fucking good. And next day, we get up, we get on an airplane and we go to Los Angeles and we play the Whisky a Go Go, which is totally fucking documented. Shows went fucking great. I mean, they went *good*. You know the band was very hot, competent. Jerry was competent. Again, we probably played faster than we ever played. We had the whole repertoire. We did a TV show. Went to SF, came back, did this, that, and other things happened there. This is where Johnny met Sable.

Sylvain Sylvain: Oh yeah, they got together and that was the end of that, you know? So we were having a great time. Playing six sold-out nights at the Whisky a Go Go… I had never been to the West Coast before. So it was my first time. And it was great, it was really cool, you know?

Nina Antonia: It's very sweet, the Johnny-Sable thing, because she's there in LA, looking at pictures of Johnny in New York, and he's in New York, sort of reading the LA rock press and seeing pictures of Sable, this superstar groupie….

Sylvain Sylvain: There were two magazines at the time: One out of New York, *Rock Scene*, by Lisa and Richard Robinson, which featured a lot of the new bands. And on the West Coast, they had *Star* magazine. Sable Starr said that they used to get *Rock Scene* and they used to say, "Man, I want to fuck this guy when he comes to LA." These were the girls in Los Angeles that were hanging out in Rodney Bingenheimer's English Disco (and it's the famous Rodney Bingenheimer, the DJ). Anyway, although me and Johnny had girlfriends in New York, we would get *Star* magazine and we would say, "Holy shit, look at this one, man! She's hot, man." At the end of the day, we want to get chicks, you know? We got the makeup from our girlfriends to get even more girlfriends!

And so they're out there so when we land at the airport. Poor Arthur he's got his thumb in a cast. When they saw him like that they said, "What happened to you?" "Oh my girlfriend did it…" "Oh, forget this guy…." So that leaves him to drink even more, you know? David can't mess around because he's with Cyrinda, so me, Johnny and Jerry we get all the girls. They meet us at the airport, Sable Starr, Lori Lightning, and who else? I don't know, but anyway we all wind up in a limousine.

We all go to the Hyatt Hotel, which was called the Rock 'n' Roll Hyatt. Johnny and Sable, they go to his room, have sex, and they're 'married.' With me, you know how hotels have adjoining doors… I looked at my room and I said, "Wow, it's open…" The housekeeping personnel never closed that door, and the room next to me was a suite. So I took it, and I was there with Lori Lightning. She was my honey at the moment. She said that she was 18, but I think she was like 13. She was going out with Jimmy Page, so I figured, she must have experience. It's rock 'n' roll.

BOB GRUEN: I was there when Johnny and Sable met. When we went to California, I went there with the Dolls. We flew in together; I was filming the whole thing. We walked into the lobby of the Continental Hyatt House, which was known as the Continental Riot House; Led Zeppelin made it kind of famous, riding motorcycles up and down the hallways.

It was pretty normal that there were groupies around. I had been there already with a couple of other bands. I was there with Alice Cooper, and Suzi Quatro…and I had been to the Hyatt House before—but never like the New York Dolls. We walked in and there must have been 30 or 40 girls just waiting in the lobby to meet the band. I think Rodney Bingenheimer had organized to bring out all the hot young groupie girls in Los Angeles to meet the New York Dolls, and I remember Sable just went right up to

Johnny and it was almost like love at first sight. They really clicked and the next couple of days they became inseparable. They were like always holding each other, touching each other, together. I know Johnny was saying he was in love, you know, he had never felt that way before. Sable, too. A few days later, after one of their shows I remember we went to Rodney's E Club and Sable actually took the microphone and announced her retirement from being the head of the groupies in Los Angeles because she was now going steady with Johnny Thunders, and she wasn't going to be available to any of the other rock stars. Johnny was her guy, and they were in love. And they were really physically in touch with each other the whole time. And they came back to New York together. I know there was a bit of a controversy; I think Sable was underage.

PETER JORDAN: I've said the line once and I'll say it again: He met Sable. Their eyes met. Their loins locked, and that was it. He fell in love overnight. They became a couple, and he sort of inherited Iggy Pop as a brother-in-law. Now this is where, depending on whom you talk to, things start to get a little bit dodgy. This is where Johnny started dibbing and dabbing. Probably where he first took some smack. It didn't manifest itself for a long period of time.

SYLVAIN SYLVAIN: Sable's sister, Coral Shield, was going out with Iggy and they all team up together and they stay at Johnny's room, cause Iggy Pop had no bread. He was hardly working. It was really us who gave him gigs to open up for us, and we played the Palladium and we played a lot of places in Los Angeles. We took him on the road. In Memphis, Tennessee, the vice squad comes to see the two bands—you know, which is The Stooges and the New York Dolls—and David Johansen gets arrested for inciting a riot; [he] invites the crowd to the stage. All four of them, the two sisters and Iggy and Johnny, were staying in Johnny's room. And Iggy became like Johnny's father-in-law—I mean, excuse me, *brother*-in-law—in a way, you know?

NINA ANTONIA: I was told by Sylvain, by several sources, that Iggy introduced Johnny to heroin. It was the worst thing that you could do for Johnny. I can't speak for Sylvain about Johnny's excessiveness, but I can speak for Johnny being a person who was emotionally wounded and emotionally insecure, and that is probably why heroin would have been the possibly worst drug for him to take, because it masks all that turmoil, all that pain. It gives you a calmness…obviously, unfortunately, it was a place he was going to return to many times over. And plus, of course, you know, Iggy Pop was Iggy Pop. Jerry himself told me that he was sort of chipping away…. I mean, Jerry was quite a sober guy initially, that's how people perceived him and his drink was whisky, but he was chipping away with heroin and that was another thing that would eventually bring them closer together, was this shared use of heroin. But it didn't happen suddenly, and in the Dolls, it happened very gradually—as it does with any addiction. It just creeps up on you. And it would have made them co-conspirators.

PETER JORDAN: Sable and Johnny latch on to each other. If they go out, they're together. If they're not going out, they're together. If they are together, they go to the show, they stay together, and that's pretty much it. We play x number of days, I think it was a full week. We go to San Francisco. She stays in LA. We come back to LA, they're together. After we wrap up what we're doing in LA, which involves a TV show, which was recorded live, we begin a tour. He sends for/arranges with Sable, and how far her family colludes in this is hard to say, because she had an unusual family. She flies to New York and goes to stay with his sister and a lady who's a secretary at Leber-Krebs. We go on with the tour, we fly to Texas and the Texas Rangers meet us at the airport because they believe that Sable is traveling with us. Cyrinda Fox, who is David's girlfriend at the time, meets us there and she is blonde, about ten years older, but a blonde, and they mistake her for Sable and there's ensuing hilarity.

The only other amusing anecdote about that is that a Rolls-Royce was sent to pick up the band. I was going down the road in a truck. They're in the Rolls-Royce, and they get pulled over by the cops. They asked Johnny what's in his pants? He's wearing a red leather suit and when he opens his pants, he has no underwear—and let it be said here, frankly, that Johnny had a very big dick. He was an Italian stallion.

So we do the tour. Wham. This takes about three weeks. We get back to New York City, and Sable and Johnny are re-united. She gets the blessing such as it may be from her parents. Her *parent* is more accurate, because she was the matriarch. They take up housekeeping in New York. This is not something I can get too deeply into. My wife was a good friend of

Sable's and many other people. They had a difficult relationship. Johnny's very jealous. Immature. Young man. She is a free-spirited and very young woman. Essentially, they get along very well.

Johnny was obsessive about everything. Obsessive baseball as a kid, obsessive guitar player…very motivated, very driven. He starts taking amphetamines, which is not helping his mental condition. Starts to make him a little paranoid and a little tense, and we are under various pressures. We have to make a second album, there are other tours…. He cannot take Sable with him everywhere; he does not have the financial wherewithal. He is very jealous about leaving her behind, and very paranoid. At one point, Sable and my wife were staying together. He was insecure. It was exacerbated by whatever, and later he began to get into taking heroin. First on—I guess—a "Why not, what does it matter? I've done everything else" basis. And down the garden path with him and aiding and abetting him, Jerry; he and Jerry wind up hanging out together. Syl's independent. David goes his own way. Arthur's in his own world, and I am busy.

So what happens, [Johnny and Sable's] relationship starts to go bad. He gets more paranoid and abusive, and he is very controlling. He wants her pretty much to not see anybody. Stay at home. Make meatloaf and god knows what the fuck else, and she's not having any of that. She doesn't really need it. She has money. Her mother is supportive. Her mother, actually, is pretty goddamn well-off. New York's not that exciting, and the Dolls weren't making any big money either, and [compared to] so many of her acquaintances, you know…somebody like Jimmy Page has got a million bucks and a castle in England and airplane tickets.

[Johnny] started to get more and more strung out. He was young and jealous. She went away and came back. The opiates alienated him more from everybody else.

Stranded in the Jungle

MARTY THAU: In Europe, they would be aware of the Dolls and be interested in their music. In America they couldn't have cared less. The unconscious people in the wasteland of America thought they were a bunch of druggy transvestites.

PETER JORDAN: We went on a tour, the first major tour they ever did of the United States. They played Chicago, which is the headquarters of Mercury Records. Arthur was good, he came back, they played the show. Came back to the city, then we started flying out doing one-offs, here, there, here, there, and everywhere, and we started rehearsing more intensely. This is where we met Nite Bob.

NITE BOB: I started touring around spring of '74 and they did weekends. You'd leave Friday morning, you'd be back Monday. There weren't that many places for them to play, Detroit was good for them. Cleveland was good for them. LA was very good for them, New York was *great* for them, you know, but, when you start going to those other markets....

I did a festival in Florida with them when they opened up for Ike and Tina Turner, right? In a big outdoor festival. Definitely a weird, wrong booking. I did shows in Canada with them, with them opening up for Billy Preston. Audience *hated* them, you know, but what are you gonna do? You work when you can work. All these people who say they saw the Dolls, I'm like, you must have been lucky because outside of New York they didn't play that much.

We did a tour of the Midwest where Kiss was the opening act, which is pretty funny. Off we went playing Flint, Michigan and Cleveland and Detroit and then go home.

All my English friends said, "we're really sorry the way your career has collapsed from working with really good bands to working with the New York Dolls." I thought they were really wrong. I had a good time working with the Dolls, it was fun.

They drove tour managers crazy. Jim Kernutt who was their tour manager, he was an advertising executive, right. He was so taken by what they were doing that he kind of gave up his family and job and went out full time with the Dolls and pretty much destroyed his career.

MARTY THAU: They went to Texas. In different locations you could see the difference of opinion of how culturally uninformed or informed people were. It was a pretty successful tour. We started playing again in New York. At this point they're pretty hot.

PETER JORDAN: Now as we got more money, we started to rehearse in slightly better places. The best place to rehearse in the city at that time was a loft in Soho called Baggy Studios. It sounds exotic but compared to most of the dumps, this was the best dump in town. They had rugs on the floors. They had rugs on the walls. They had rugs on the ceiling. They were famous for having had this Afro-Cuban soul band Mandrill live there for a year. It was pretty funky, but it was hip and the amps were good. They had a tie-in with an amplifier company, so they had a million fucking amps. So we rehearsed there all the time and it was a good spot and the band got better.

And as we went out, we took this guy Bob Sekowsky on the road with us, and he nailed the sound down to a degree where all of a sudden, you know, against all fucking odds, we were sounding pretty good. And we went to Europe, the second time, and that's been documented in various places. There's that French film with the fight breaking out and all that. Have you seen that? And so it went pretty good. Most of it was television.

NINA ANTONIA: *The Old Grey Whistle Test* was a program for adult music fans. Sometimes you'd get a treat like Alex Harvey, but it wasn't really very much fun to sit through. So when the Dolls came on, I mean…you'd got Johnny doing that fabulous duck walk, and he's wearing that skull painted on the back of his black leather jacket, and Arthur's got his blue platform boots on, and they're making this great calamitous racket and Bob Harris…poor old Bob Harris (the presenter), with his beard and his nice dad face, chortles patronizingly at them and goes, "Hu hu hu mock rock."

That in a sense was a thrown gauntlet to the next generation. Oh god, it was Joe Strummer or Mick Jones, Paul Cook…I think everybody who was awake after bedtime that night, me included, watching *The Old Grey Whistle Test*—Morrissey as well—it was just like, "Oh god, there's this comet and it's called the New York Dolls and it's the beginning of the new era."

MARTY THAU: They did a performance at Biba's, and Malcolm showed up backstage and he loved them. But at first, he didn't know what to make of them. He thought that they were terrible. I think it was Greil Marcus, the writer—in *Lipstick Traces*, I think—he wrote about Malcolm, and how they came into his shop, and his, you know, snubbing them, thought they were ridiculous. And then he thought, "Hmm, how amazing this is! These guys are so bad, and I'm finding myself laughing along with them and liking them." A year later, he's playing Dolls records for the Sex Pistols, and saying, "You should do this and you should do that like the Dolls do it."

SYLVAIN SYLVAIN: First of all, we play Biba's in London; what an incredible show that was. As a matter of fact, Arthur Kane gets busted for switching tags on the clothing. I was with him, and it made the BBC *News* that night. Marty bails us out and is like, "No no no no, these guys are going to play here."

We get really ripped up. We were like, not used to drinking so much—especially Johnny—and as you know, in England they drink a lot. So we take the plane from London and we land at the Orly Airport in Paris. There were already people there we knew from Max's Kansas City, like Jean-Pierre Kalfon, and his friend Octavio Cohen-Escali. We were walking together down the airport hallways and the press say to us, "Welcome to Paris!" And Johnny, man, the first thing: "Bluuuuurrrrrrrr…!" He fucking *throws up*, right there in front of all the paparazzi. What a fucking scene.

And then the next thing was we play this place called The Bataclan, which is for kids, so it only costs like two francs to get in there. The place was packed. I remember looking down from the dressing room and there was a big, big crowd. I mean, you couldn't even fit another finger in there and I said, "Johnny, look, look! The Beatles must be here!" You know, cause there were so many kids outside.

On my side of the stage, I get all the drag queens and everybody else. On Johnny's side, he gets all the tough guys and the Parisian killers. I don't know what happened. One of them spit on Johnny, and Johnny fucking takes the microphone and throws it at the guy and that was it, man. A riot started. A riot. A fucking riot. Somebody there filmed it all, and then those kids on his side started getting on the stage, and we had to rush out of venue, get the hell out of there quick. If not, they were going to kill us.

I did this French interview backstage beforehand and I introduced everybody in French, and I introduced Arthur Kane—*the Monster of the band is Arthur Kane*. So we were having a great time, living it up. And then the show happened. Then the riot started. We had to get the hell out of there.

Anyway, we got back to this hotel we were staying at, the Ambassador. Jean-Pierre Kalfon nicknamed it the Ambassa*dolls*. So we're going back to the Ambassadolls, and Johnny, man, he finds this gorgeous, gorgeous girl, and she had these huge dogs. They went upstairs to the hotel room with these dogs, you know. Then we started getting phone calls, like, it's the managers and everything. They say, "This is against all our rules! We don't have no dogs in here! This is the Ambassador Hotel, Paris!" The whole night, I swear to god, they were knocking on doors to find the dogs. Of course, they never find the dogs.

The next morning, we're down in the lobby, heading into our vehicles to go to our next venue and who comes down in the elevator, with his girlfriend and the dogs? It's *Johnny*. And then they say "Where were they?" He's got this big smile on his face.

There was this Parisian drag queen. Her name was Marie France. If you ever see that photograph of me and David on the bed? Like it's a post-card. Anyway, we were sharing a room and Marie France was up there for a while. Her and David were kind of chatting up…I don't know what else happened. I am not at liberty to tell ya, but you can ask David if he remembers. But she was incredible looking. So we had all these things, man, in Paris, which was great. Malcolm McLaren and Vivienne Westwood came. We played the Olympia Theatre. My mother Marcelle started having respect for her son being a musician 'cause we grew up in Paris, and anybody that would play the Olympia Theatre was like Charles Aznavour and Edith

Piaf. They were huge, huge stars, and so when she found out that her son played the Olympia Theatre, she was calling up my uncle and all my relatives. I earned her respect on that. She always did support me, but I had a tough time convincing my parents…well, we all did, you know.

NINA ANTONIA: The Dolls get to Orly Airport and Johnny is sick in front of the French press—he vomits. Jerry Nolan described it: "Johnny was as sick as dog in front of the cameras." Is that punk rock? I mean, it's two things. Malcolm McLaren sees that, and the reaction of the press, and would adapt it for the Sex Pistols, but it's also…is that Johnny being junk sick for the first time? We don't know, but there you go. It becomes an iconic moment in retelling the Dolls' story, but also, McLaren's brain is really fired up by them. He's prepared to follow them to the ends of the earth and to leave restaurants with bills unpaid because of the New York Dolls.

MARTY THAU: They played the Olympia Theatre, which to me was a highlight, because I knew of this theater from days earlier, when Edith Piaf and Gilbert Bécaud appeared there. And these were sensational shows that are classic, that are there for all time in history, and the Dolls really did it.

For the first couple of songs, the audience didn't know what to make of it. They were sitting there, kind of quiet. And all of a sudden, Johnny Thunders takes the front to do "Chatterbox." This woke everybody up, and they rushed the stage. He had such a presence. His solo performances… his performances as the lead singer were always very awakening. There was always an awakening of the audience when he would get to that. Maybe that was, you know, part of the conclusion on his part that he could be a solo artist successfully.

I remember that this one time in Paris, they were staying at the Ambassador, which is a pretty elegant hotel. There was a press conference, and because of the fact that the Dolls were doing a very limited amount of performances in Europe, these journalists were coming from all around Europe. They got there to do this major press conference and the Dolls were scheduled to show up at four o'clock. But the Dolls didn't show up at four o'clock. They didn't show up at five o'clock and they didn't show up at six o'clock. And when I started seeing that this was not going to happen, I

PHOTO: YANN MERCADER

didn't want to lose this crowd, so I declared an open bar—and by the time the Dolls *did* show up, these journalists were drunk out of their heads.

Everybody gets light and loose, and it seems that (the Dolls) were upstairs in the company of members of the Communist Party, one or two press figures, local musicians, beautiful starlets…this was the welcoming committee to Paris. They finally came down. They did this press conference in front of this drunken crowd and it was very successful.

I'll give you an example of something: When they recorded their album, it cost $17,000. Do you know how cheap that is? I mean, bands were making records for $50, $100, $150,000. The Dolls were *zap!* In. Out. $17,000 was very frugal. That was very capable. They liked to be treated to a dinner from time to time, but that is the responsibility of a record company to take care of things like that, to treat their artists in a stylistic fashion. The open bar bill at the Ambassador Hotel for the press came to $8,000. Now, I don't think for all the press value that they got out of it, across Europe, $8,000 was minuscule. If you wanted to buy all that press, it would have cost you a lot more.

NITE BOB: When I first started touring with them they said, "OK you're going to room with Johnny." That's no worries, right? Well that lasted about two days. When he'd unpack his bag, a nuclear bomb went off in the room. Clothes everywhere.

And their management trying to keep them, you know, kind of stable. We wouldn't get per diem, cash money for expenses. You could sign like $15 a day to your hotel room, right, so I'd check out of my room the first day and there'd be $150 worth of liquor signed to the room—to my name! Their management would encourage them to be outrageous, to be late, you know, to make a mark. Be different from everybody else. There was a balance between chaos and order all the time.

Too Much Too Soon

MARTY THAU: My preference was for Jerry Leiber and Mike Stoller to produce the second album. And they said, "Yes, we'll do it." And then as time got closer and closer, they said, "We can't do it." For whatever reason, they were busy. They were administering an empire of songs; they had Red Bird Records, The Dixie Cups, Stealers Wheel. Everything they touched was successful. Then they said, "But we can recommend someone: Shadow Morton." George Shadow Morton, who would probably do a great job. I didn't think that they would tell me something like that unless they really meant it, because they were pretty serious people. I said, "Okay, would you please tell Shadow Morton to contact me?" We met, and I even took him to Chicago to Mercury to meet Irwin Steinberg, and got him a deal there with them for something separate, so he was pretty happy. He went into the studio, and he didn't know what to make of [the Dolls]. He went out on the road with them to see upfront what this was all about. And by the time we got back to New York and ready to do an album, he was well versed in what the Dolls were about.

NINA ANTONIA: The second album is even more important than the first album, because there's more on the table. They've had moderate sales; they need to have better sales. They're a high-risk band. They're expensive to run. Mercury are a little bit nervous of them, so it's gotta be a great album. And so they get in Shadow Morton. And Shadow Morton, as we know, had worked with The Shangri-Las.

NITE BOB: There was that girl-group influence in that band. [Shadow] produced all those records that were meaningful. They used a hip producer for the first record, right? Maybe they wanted to go more rootsier with Shadow Morton. I didn't go to any of those sessions. I was out on tour with another band at that time. To me it was still the Dolls, where you could see like a slight fragmentation starting to happen. The first album is kind of consistent, then you can see this is more David's song. This is more of a Johnny thing, you know? Like "Chatterbox" versus "Human Being."

LENNY KAYE: I thought the choice of Shadow Morton was interesting. Here's a person who knows how to capture drama and a sense of theatre, which is what the Dolls were about. They probably didn't have as much time to write a whole new album as they did with the first album. This is pretty common. Sophomore jinx—where, unless you are really attentive, you have a shorter amount of time to come up with *x* amount of songs. I always think that the two albums are like heads and tails. There's really not a lot of difference between the two. Second one has "Babylon." First one has "Personality Crisis." It's still pretty much the Dolls. They didn't really advance that well. With the first one, they played most of their hits, and the second one, they are experimenting a little bit. I think Shadow Morton tried to understand that, even though he was outside their social circle—and maybe that was why he was brought in. I think it's not so much a Shadow Morton production as say, the Dolls setting up again and going for their "live" flavor. There is a little bit of extra keyboards, and a little bit of horn here and there...but really it's pretty much the New York Dolls, you know. Here we are. Take us or leave us.

BOB GRUEN: Shadow is a cool guy, a mysterious guy. He kind of floated around. He was in the corners—he was in the shadows. But he was a great producer. He let the band do what they wanted, and *helped* them do what they wanted to do. There's a lot of people who criticize the quality of the records, and it's the only record we have of what the Dolls were like. Personally, when they came out, I liked them, and all their fans liked them. I thought the albums were pretty good. We played them a lot.

SYLVAIN SYLVAIN: The guitars were overdubbed like Johnny's, and he gave it that kind of razor sound that now becomes punk—whatever you want to call it. You know—music. And he did great on that. But the songs were already written. They were already hits. All the songs that we passed on [for] the first album became the second album, cause we only wrote two new songs on the second album—which was "Puss in Boots" and "Babylon." Everything else was oldies. They decided, let's pay more attention to David and try to make David whatever he was.… It wasn't like a group effort anymore. I love the second album—it's a great album. I'll be glad to take anything The New York—the original New York Dolls—would ever give us.

Nina Antonia: What's important to me about *Too Much Too Soon* is "Chatterbox," because each thing, you can see what's leading to the next. Now Johnny really had to fight to get that track on there, and to play that song at shows as well, because I think David Johansen thought, "What am I supposed to do, just play my tambourine?" But that's Johnny's moment, "Chatterbox." It's the best song on the album, because it absolutely rocks it apart.

Nite Bob: They had started to change musically. 'Cause they'd grown. They'd gone out and they'd played a lot of shows. They became like, a little more bluesier. There was much more blues influence in that record. To me I thought it was also kind of fragmented. I think there were some songs on there that were left over from the initial period. The energy was there, but it's…it's tough to look back, you know, say 40-some odd years and say, "What would have happened if…?" I don't know, you know? It's a documentation of that point in time of what they are capable of doing.

Sylvain Sylvain: The second album really became like the first David Johansen solo album. The girls singing background music in "Stranded in the Jungle": "Chew-wop-a-bop-bop.…" They were gorgeous, man, and they sounded great. But it was not the little campiness that me and Johnny could have put on there. And doing it like the way we did it—live, on *Don Kirshner's Rock Concert*—which was really more the New York Dolls. And it became more and more of that, and less and less, you know.… I mean, I even had a hard time in putting "Great god Sugar Mooga, let me out of here!" on "Stranded in the Jungle." David didn't want that. He said, "It's there already." I said, "Yeah, but it's my little shtick." I wrote the song "Too

Much Too Soon," and they didn't have time to do it. It's not Shadow's fault. It's management, LSD (Lead Singer Disease), and on and on. It's a great album; we appreciate anything the New York Dolls gave us on their first journey.

MARTY THAU: He went into the studio. He brought in some great background singers—Ellie Greenwich, and you know, a couple of others—but it was out of character. There was not enough original material. There were too many oldies on the record. They were done well. I mean "There's Gonna Be a Showdown" was a hot track. I thought it was good. I thought it could have been a little bit better. In terms of comparing Rundgren to Morton, I think I'd have to say that Rundgren was a little cooler. Shadow did a good job. Shadow was the man of mystery. He was rumored to be married to two different people at the same time. I don't know if that's true or not.

PETER JORDAN: Second album was good; I happened to really enjoy it. The tours that we did were good. But the records weren't selling.

SYLVAIN SYLVAIN: Well, the sales weren't very good on the first one; they sold 80,000 records. The second one sold less, but we weren't number one —that's definite. Although our songs were hits to our fans, and they still sell every year to new kids that come around. They saying that we never sold a million copies? That's bullshit. I don't believe it. Not after all these years. But anyway, at the time they came out, they weren't successful and we were on salary.

MARTY THAU: I think they shipped 90,000 records to begin with, and they thought with all the press, that this band was going to go gold overnight. This was going to be an overnight immediate sensation. I thought, well, if they ship 90 and they sell another 50, I'd be thrilled.

So I am in Chicago and they're telling me, "Ah, we're really disappointed." And I said, "Let me ask you something: How many other artists on your label sold 90,000 or shipped 90,000 the first time around and received as much international press as the Dolls?" Setting them up for, you know, the next record and the next record? They never answered because it shot down their whole theory about underselling. It was not true. I think they shipped a little bit less on the second record.

But I also knew that they'd gone to Cleveland and they'd play and there'd be…not a sold-out crowd, but let's say 70% of the auditorium would fill up. Then we'd go back five months later and it would be sold out. And I thought wow, if this is what's going to happen, what we have to do is we have to go into each city, and then we have to go *back* to each city, and if we have to go back a *third* time, we'll go back.

I remember playing New Year's Eve in Detroit and selling like three thousand tickets. That was the biggest Dolls payday. I remember walking out of there with a paper bag with $13,000 in cash, and going back to the hotel and checking it in to the safe just for safe-keeping. That was the strategy. That was the reality. That was what we had to do. This was not going to be something that was going to happen overnight. And as long as I believed in it, that satisfied me; *I'll just keep going until it happens.* I believed. And I was following my own instincts.

NINA ANTONIA: Well, *Too Much Too Soon* did okay, but it didn't do better than their debut, and I think that's when Mercury started to get really nervous. The band was imploding. I mean, Arthur was a heavy drinker. Johnny and Jerry had sort of separated from David and Sylvain, so this rift had developed. And David and Johnny were the principal songwriters, but they weren't communicating as well anymore. So it's like, where do we go from here?

MARTY THAU: What troubled me was, I had to have the support of the label. They had to believe what they were being told, which was accurate reflection on my part and Steve Leber's part. They had to believe that and go along with it until it happened. It could have taken another two years. It could have taken another two albums. But it was going to happen.

NITE BOB: When a band isn't moving forward, people start pointing the finger. When people are unhappy, they try to make themselves happy, you know? A lot of people think the Dolls were like this drugged-out band, and they weren't that bad, really. I mean, it was soft. When you don't have any money, you really kind of depend on the kindness of strangers, you know. Artie, sometimes…he'd drink a little too much, and he'd be a little bit wobbly and…. There was one point in Cleveland where the band left the stage and Arthur didn't realize the song was over. [He] kept playing, and the audience took it as some kind of bass solo, you know? And he just kept going. And the band's on the side of the stage, going, like, "might as well go back out…" and they just picked up where they left off.

You're either going up or you're going down. And the gigs got worse and worse. We played a bunch of gigs in Detroit in a shopping mall, right? And then people start to doubt the project. Especially Jerry and Johnny. I think they were looking to do something harder musically.

Marty Thau: David and Syl were not unreliable at all. They were not tee-totalers, let's get that straight. They did their share of carousing, [but] not Syl so much. David was a serious drinker, but they took care of business. Jerry Nolan was pretty quiet and off to the side. But Johnny was doing drugs at that point. They were unreliable because of Johnny; he was the main source of getting stoned. When I learned that Jerry also was taking drugs, I said, "You fool. You're 28 years old. You have a new, good gig, you know, and you're taking drugs? It's going to lead you down." Johnny did try on a number of occasions to stop taking drugs, but he just couldn't pull it off. He would always revert back to it. And I thought to myself, *I can't depend on these guys. I have a wife and kids to support and mortgages to pay. If I can't depend on these guys, this is just a waste of time.* And I warned them of this. I called a meeting of the Dolls and Leber and myself. We were down in this bar, in this dark bar, sitting in the back, and I said, "Look guys, if you can't get your act together, there's no way that you can succeed. Not only that: There's no way, if you don't get your act together, I wanna be involved with you, because you'll make it impossible for me to earn money. You'll be too unreliable." They listened, but they couldn't get rid of their demons and…I left.

Sylvain Sylvain: They were thinking of dropping us from Mercury after *Too Much Too Soon.* I wrote this song called "Teenage News." In the eyes of a lot of people—writers and managers—this was finally the song that was going to become a big hit. I talked to Leber. He said that Marty Thau was out. He wanted us to record "Teenage News," and he was going to take us to Japan on a tour. We were going to make money, finally. We're going to have a hit record, and we'll proceed.

First of all, we tried to make a demo. Jack Douglas came to my apartment on Charles Street in Greenwich Village and I played him "Teenage News." He loved it. He said, "Okay, we're in the studio." We go to the studio and who's next door? John Lennon. I knew John already, because I was in one of the John and Yoko movies—*Up Your Legs Forever*. They filmed you from your toes to your waist; it was an art movie. I got paid a dollar in 1968. I'm number 400, if you want to catch my great performance.

I love The Beatles and The Rolling Stones and all those bands, but of course, The Beatles and John Lennon…. John Lennon was to me the most important part of The Beatles besides Ringo Starr. So yeah, I see John Lennon. He's next door. He's in the small studio and we're in the big studio. He was making that *Rock 'n' Roll* album. And I had my big white Falcon. You know, the Gretsch—the Cadillac. It's not a guitar, really; it's a Cadillac.

So I said, "Hey, I was in your movie—you know, *Up Your Legs Forever*." He said, "Oh you were? Oh man…." And we start talking about the Dolls and I said, "Come on over to the room, check out the white Gretsch. I have this beautiful guitar you're gonna love." And then he picked it up. He was playing my white Gretsch. This was great.

We started demoing "Teenage News." Johnny never showed up. Too fucked up. Jerry did show up. Arthur Kane never showed up, but Peter was there. So we demo that song. I don't think we ever finished it. I don't think it ever got off the ground. Word got back to Leber that they couldn't cut it, so he takes us out to these guys named [Jerry] Kasenetz and [Jeff] Katz. They were big producers at the time, making bubblegum music. They take me and David out to this big studio in Long Island and they played us a record and they said, "This is going to be your next big hit. You don't have to sing it. You don't have to play it. You don't have to do anything. All you gotta do is sign right here." And then we just flip out.

And then I just say, "I need a ride back to New York," and that's the end of that. I think David was in shock. And I said that was it, you know?

NINA ANTONIA: I have a flyer here for a show that they do at this point, and it's advertising a free buffet. It's an incentive which is kind of really sad. Can you imagine the New York Dolls having to play buffet shows and get welfare? That's right at the end where Malcolm comes in with his red-patent-leather rescue package.

Red Patent Leather

SYLVAIN SYLVAIN: One day I'm walking down in front of the Chelsea Hotel, on 23ʳᵈ Street in New York, and coming out of the lobby is Malcolm McLaren. And I said, "Hey man, what's happening? What are you doing?" He says, "How's the Dolls, mate?" "Ah, pretty fucked up. We're about to break up." And he says, "Oh man, I loved the band. Is there anything I could do, man? I would do it for you." And I say, "If you want to, yeah." And that's how the whole thing got started.

He rented this loft right down the road on 23ʳᵈ Street, and we started doing the whole *Red Patent Leather* show. It was because of a song that me and David wrote, this song called "Red Patent Leather." It was: "Red, you're the judge, Red, you're the jury, Red, you're the executioner." It was a little bit political, because we did have an agenda. It wasn't just music, folks! Or nice shoes. But we were not Communists. Just like we weren't Nazis when Johnny Thunders wore swastikas. We saw Brian Jones doing it, we said, "Holy shit!" You know? "That's cool." I'm a Jewish Kid. When we came to America, my mother said to me, "Don't tell anybody you're a Jew. That's how we were going to survive." So I said, oh good. This guy's going to wear swastikas. That's fantastic. They'll never think I'm a Jew. And that's how it was. It's unfortunate, but she was trying to protect me. We weren't Nazis or communists.

PETER JORDAN: They would constantly go with a litany of different things that they needed. Be it scams, or just outright "I need money for rent. I need money for this. I need clothes." Arthur never got it together to do any of that. Subsequently, he felt short-changed in many respects. But he had alienated himself too, through heavy drinking. Everyone had various problems. Meanwhile, I'm kind of navigating down the middle. David always had the management behind him, and he was pretty stable in that he stayed in one place. And he would ask for money, and he would get it. Syl was more of a hustler. Johnny and Jerry started to need more money cause they needed more money, and eventually the pot was not going anywhere. Either they had to really buckle down and tour like a motherfucker, or start to make a lot of cuts—and that wasn't happening in their mind.

They had their own side of the story. Johnny was writing material. Jerry never wrote anything. I mean, he might have written a song or two long after he left the band, but Johnny was writing more. Subsequently, he wanted to sing more. So that was not going to work out either, because, as David once told me (and we had a discussion): "I'm not going to play tambourine." You know? So it was starting to fall apart there, but that was only one of a million little nitpicks. And it just started to come down.

Eventually Leber and Krebs ran out of money that they were going to spend. They were making a lot of money from other acts, but the other acts were doing everything! You know, jumping through a hoop. Aerosmith started out making money and just kept making money. The Dolls were losing money. Are they [Leber and Krebs] the villains, or not? Could they have been more understanding? They just told us, "We're not giving you any more money. Get your shit together." Etcetera.

So at that point, again, we started rehearsing like crazy. I rehearsed with Johnny and Jerry. We had a whole shitload of songs. Arthur was going in and out of rehab, so I was learning the songs. It used to be that Arthur would learn the songs, he'd teach them to me. Then I was learning the songs and teaching them to Arthur! And this was going nowhere, because Arthur couldn't fucking play them.

But everyone was loyal; there was a certain loyalty there. They were not going to fire Arthur. He wasn't going to go anywhere. That wasn't an option; I couldn't even bring it up. I was like, "Why the fuck don't I play the songs, we have Arthur play the tambourine?" That wasn't happening, so we did this whole build-up to this *Red Patent Leather* thing, which was meant to be a goof, and Arthur was supposed to play. He had the costume. He had everything. The night before he was supposed to play, he went in rehab, again. So I wound up playing, wearing his suit. And then a week later, *Jerry* had to go into fucking rehab, and we used this guy Spider, from the band called Pure Hell.

NITE BOB: David Krebs used to say they were great in a club setting, but they weren't able to step up when they get over 1,000 people. And that was kind of true. It was hard to spread that energy to the back of a big room, and they really couldn't rise above that small club level. And you know they didn't get picked up for a third record. They rehearsed for a third record. There were songs ready to go and we did shows in LA that producers came to and all that, and then it all kind of went sideways.

MARTY THAU: They were still under contract to me and Leber and they weren't going anywhere, so when Malcolm showed up, they were in the last ten minutes of their existence. Malcolm couldn't pull it off anyway. He didn't know enough about the music business, and they saw through him.

BOB GRUEN: Under the management of Leber-Krebs, the band was doing pretty well; they were on a salary. The management was giving them money to pay their rent and get by. Every time they played a gig it was completely sold out, but the audience would go crazy and literally jump up and down on the seats, start fights with each other…. Some guys were trying to get out, some guys were trying to get to the stage; so they'd be fighting in the audience. They'd be standing on the seats. Seats would get broken.

And pretty soon, even though they were on the cover of a lot of magazines, they were the most notorious band in the country, a lot of promoters didn't want to book them because it was just too much trouble. You couldn't get insurance for a band like that, because the theaters were getting broken. Doors were getting smashed because there was too many people trying to get in…seats were getting smashed, you know? It was just total chaos. Now for an audience member, that might be fun. But for somebody who actually has to be responsible for the theater, it wasn't fun at all. So it was getting harder and harder to book them. So they weren't really making much money. They weren't selling a lot of records.

There was a lot of drinking going on. Arthur drank more than anybody I've ever seen in my life. Johnny and Jerry discovered heroin and that takes a lot of time, and so instead of the show being 20 minutes late or half an hour late, it started being an hour late or an hour and a half late. Being two hours late is too late. When you're supposed to play at 9:00 and the band hasn't even gotten to the theater at 10:30 and the audience is sitting out there…. People come to a show, they have drinks, they take drugs, they're ready to rock at 9:00; by 11:00, they're kind of coming down already, and *then* the band would come out. So it was really dysfunctional.

Eventually, Leber-Krebs thought they weren't going to make any money with the band. They were spending too much money and they weren't getting any back, and so they stopped managing the band. And it was just about then that Malcolm McLaren showed up with a whole set of clothes that he had made for the band. Now the band had gone to England in the fall and they had gone into Malcolm's store and they got along. And Malcolm really liked them, and he thought they were exciting and interesting and new and he liked the controversy of them…. Malcolm is an artist, and his art was all about chaos, confusion and controversy. He talked to each band member about making a special set of clothes for them and each guy got to design his own style. David had a gabardine suit. A couple of them had some leather outfits and some of the pants or jackets were made out of plastic or had a vest. They were all individual designs but in the same bright, bright red. Like fire-engine-red color. And so Malcolm came to New York basically to bring the clothes and have the New York Dolls wear them. He was surprised when he got here to find out that the band was basically breaking up. That the management had dropped them—they had no management. They had no shows booked. They had nothing, actually.

It was early winter, like January or so of '75. The band was basically over, but Malcolm had all these clothes and he wanted them to wear his clothes and make some publicity for him. So it wasn't like he became the manager of the New York Dolls. He kind of organized some shows so they would wear his clothes. And he gets a lot of credit for being "the manager" of the Dolls, but he didn't create the Dolls. He came in at the end. What Malcolm did was save their lives, because they were so down and out.

Johnny and Jerry had pretty severe heroin habits. Arthur was drinking more than anybody I had ever seen. I remember in California one day I walked into his room when he woke up, and he had bottle of peppermint schnapps next to his bed and he just drank about half the bottle, the way a person would drink a bottle of water, you know, when they wake up. Malcolm put Arthur into Roosevelt Hospital into a detox unit there and he got Jerry and Johnny into a kind of drug detox situation to clean them up a bit. It did save their lives and he cleaned them up enough that they played a couple of shows at the Hippodrome on the East Side. Two weekends—I think they were held over for a third weekend by popular demand. It was the last time they played in New York. They were really chaotic. By the third week, Johnny and Jerry were having their problems. Arthur was so drunk he was having trouble playing. Peter Jordan was standing in for Arthur. I think this guy named Spider from Philadelphia came up and he was playing drums instead of Jerry, and it was really kind of falling apart.

NINA ANTONIA: Enter Malcolm McLaren with this rescue package, because he loved the Dolls so much. He didn't want to see them go to the wall without his idea for re-launching them as sort of the rent-boy division of the Chinese Red Guard. It was really quite funny. They're all creaking around in this very thick sort of patent leather. The material that he used is so thick, it's like industrial strength rubber. It must have been very difficult to walk in.

SYLVAIN SYLVAIN: We were all sitting in the loft and one guy would come up: "Hey man, I want to get red shoes. You think Vivienne will make me red shoes, Malcolm?" "Oh yeah, yeah." Then the other guy said, "Wait a minute, I want red shoes, too." Okay. We're all going to get red shoes. Okay. Great. You know and then, "Hey, do you think she'll make me red pants?" "Yeah, yeah, okay." "Man, great. Okay. Now we'll all get...let's all go red." "Okay, great."

David and Malcolm never really had a good rapport, but there was this one second together when David said, "Why don't we put up the red flag?" Malcolm is a little bit of a commie bastard—*pinko bastard*, as I would like to call him. No, he's the sweetest guy. I love Malcolm. But still, he *is* a fucking pinko bastard, and he always had a little bit of a political agenda. But we did too, in a way. Where we're pointing fingers with "Vietnamese Baby," which marks our stand against the Vietnam War. It was David Johansen's tune, which me and Johnny Thunders T. Rexed the shit out of.

NITE BOB: Malcolm was Malcolm, you know? He had some good concepts, but he was deathly afraid of everybody, 'cause we were hard New York people. We'd always be threatening to beat him up because he had these fluffy sweaters. The red patent leather was probably another bad turn for them, the hammer-and-sickle backdrop. I think it may have been a poor choice at that time.

McLaren was kind of experimenting with them, and then took aspects of it and then worked it into the Sex Pistols. He needed people who were a little younger, who could take…who would *listen* to him, because the Dolls would sometimes *not* listen to him. They'd given up on their previous management and they were looking for someone to save them. It was just shrinking, failing, and tail-spinning out at that point. That's when things started to get bad.

LEEE BLACK CHILDERS: I didn't know who Malcolm McLaren was; I'd never heard of him. I was off with Mott the Hoople by this time, and Iggy Pop. I'd branched out, I had all these bands. I'm winging my way all across America, and someone rings me on the phone—I think it was Lisa Robinson—and she said, "Can you believe what's happened? Malcolm McLaren has dressed 'em up in red clothes and they're Communists now." She went "Ha ha ha," you know? My major artist [David Bowie] is a space alien! This is cool. All right, we're fine. I should make some more money and eat some more crepes, and I didn't pay any attention to it. But apparently it was bad. Decisions were being made while I was off, nothing to do with me at all.

SYLVAIN SYLVAIN: Lisa Robinson calls me up. She said, "You guys tried the fag thing, didn't work." Not that we tried anything like that, but anyway, we did kind of do a drag show—the only drag show—at the Club 82, which was a drag house at number 82 East 4th Street, by the way. (That's the address in the basement.) And she said, "Now you're going to go Communist??" She didn't get it. Nobody really got it. And yes, it was the end of the war and it was a bad moment and we were fucking schmucks, but we were just the creative kids and we believed whatever we wanted to do should be seen and should be heard. And it wasn't that we were out to shock. We weren't; we weren't that clever. We were just real. We thought this is our next move and yeah, we have that song "Red Patent Leather." It worked until later on, when people heard about it. But it worked at the time we did the Little Hippodrome.

LENNY KAYE: My take on the Malcolm McLaren red leather/hammer when I saw them at the Hippodrome: I thought that both [parties] were thinking too conceptually. Malcolm getting some of the ideas he would later take into the Sex Pistols—the presentation, the shock value, the sense of manipulation. For the Dolls: A sense of desperation, because they had played their cards, and what were they going to do next? And, of course, by this time, drugs were rampant within the group, and that's not good for any creative spirit.

Seeing the Dolls in that period was seeing an era in transition, because you've also lost the glam rock scene that was part of New York in the early '70s, and it's moved over to a club called CBGB, where the style of dress is different and the attitude is different and the presentation is different. Band generations happen very quickly, especially in an accelerated city like New York. So by 1974, it's a new day. The Dolls, I'm sure, felt like, "What are all these upstarts coming up, when we haven't even really made it ourselves?" So for me, that smacked of desperation. It was too well conceived.

The early Dolls had different personalities; Johnny had his kind of cowboy bouffant, and Syl really did look like a doll, and David, who's moving back and forth between the genders, and Jerry who's always the guy behind the drums—no matter what he was wearing—and Arthur is the space cadet. They all had little different things. It wasn't as unified as this red patent leather look. I thought it was a little forced, myself, and I wasn't surprised when it kind of started falling apart immediately after.

NINA ANTONIA: Cyrinda Foxe stayed up all night sewing a Communist Flag for this great red re-launch, and David comes out reading the words of Chairman Mao. I mean, it was spectacular. But was it spectacular in the right way? For me, what's important, I think, was Johnny did "Pirate Love." You know, so each stage of the game you can see where it's going to, and he's still really tight with Jerry....

I think a lot of people were a little dumbfounded by the red-patent-leather revamp.

NITE BOB: I mean, they were all wearing these red patent-leather suits. If Artie couldn't play, you'd slide Peter on, 'cause he looked right and he knew all the songs. They were fighting to survive at that point. Every gig was important to them.

SYLVAIN SYLVAIN: The *Red Patent Leather* show I recorded on my little Studer-Revox was never supposed to be released as an album...and I released it! With Marty Thau. Everybody got one fifth of whatever we got as an advance.

MARTY THAU: The *"new"* New York Dolls…. Malcolm even put out a press release calling Leber and Krebs and me "paper tigers." I was pissed off, but I thought, *Anybody who burns their bridges like that is destined to lose.* He tried to enforce his situationist theory, political theory, onto the press of New York. Who the hell is this guy? Comes in to New York and he's telling us how to politically think.

RICHARD LLOYD: Malcolm wanted to make a big splash, and there was this place on 56th Street. It was quite famous, like a Copacabana, where usually you had Spanish and Hispanic salsa. He called our manager and said, would Television like to do a double-headlining gig with the Dolls? We agreed to it, and we were fine with going on first because then we could leave earlier. But they were wearing red leather and behind them they had a huge hammer and sickle…. This is before glasnost, so it was very, very, very strange.

Malcolm fell in love with Television and our look. Richard Hell was still in the band. Malcolm asked if he could manage us. Tom was ostensibly the leader of the band. We used to vote. There was a voting if he could manage us—"We're not interested." Malcolm picked out Richard Hell and thought he was the star, and Tom couldn't deal with that. So he said, "I'm going to say no." And I looked at him like he's crazy, and I said, "But this man's like a con man. He's like a Colonel Tom Parker. I mean, if we went with him, we might be millionaires in a month."

Tom could be very funny. He looked at me and he said, "Do you wanna end up in red leather?"

Now I didn't find out 'til a lot later that that was not Malcolm that thought of that. Malcolm saw The Ramones, he saw us, he was managing the Dolls as they were collapsing. And he called his wife Vivienne—who had SEX, the fashion store—and he talked about the ripped clothing and what in hindsight I would call the *glamour of poverty*. I mean, we looked like hobos, children from the future or from another planet, with torn clothes and like, tits showing. Malcolm told his wife about it. Of course, she couldn't just sell an old T-shirt that it's falling apart, so she began adding zippers and safety pins, and Malcolm went back and created the Sex

Pistols. Primarily the energy of the Dolls and the Ramones, and the look of Television—that was the Sex Pistols.

SYLVAIN SYLVAIN: Malcolm *loved* Richard Hell. He left me a suit and he said to me, "Sylvain, you've got to give this to Richard." He loved Richard.

ANDY SHERNOFF: Drugs were separating the band. I'm saying this from the outside, but if you're doing heroin and you're a junkie, you're only hanging out with other junkies. You're not really interested in people who aren't doing drugs, because your whole life is about copping and the next fix. Of course it interferes with the music. McLaren made a valiant attempt to rescue the Dolls, but I think it was in the cards that it was going to fall apart.

SYLVAIN SYLVAIN: One day Malcolm McLaren brings this map of the United States to the loft on 23rd Street, and he starts putting little pins on it. He said, "First we played the Little Hippodrome. Then we go to Florida to play, and then we come back to play The Beacon Theatre." The Beacon Theatre on 75th Street? 76th Street? Right around there. Broadway. Big theater. Nice theater. So we're going to make our little comeback. It all worked until we break up in Florida. Staying at Jerry Nolan's mother's house.

NITE BOB: They were going to do those shows in Florida, and I didn't go because Pete Jordan said, "Don't go. 'Cause I don't know if we'll get back." The band was fragmented. The shows were getting worse and worse. When they had stronger management [Leber-Krebs], there was money. When they split from them, there was no money. They somehow got some plane tickets to go down there and do it. That's when the band completely imploded. I was glad I wasn't there. 'Cause I did like them as people, and as a band. It's really tough to watch people disintegrate.

PETER JORDAN: Things were getting kind of bad. Then they fire me. And they're going to go take Arthur out of rehab and go down to Florida and start a tour with no roadie and Malcolm driving them. They're there 24 hours and Johnny calls me again. He said, "Come down. Arthur can't play." So I go down. That lasted for two weeks.

MARTY THAU: Arthur is getting DT's, delirium tremens, in the morning; he's getting the shakes. Johnny and Jerry are shooting up. How could they possibly succeed when 60 percent of them are unreliable and stoned out of their heads? No way. I knew I had made the right decision. Aside from the fact that it couldn't support my lifestyle, which was carefully managed.

SYLVAIN SYLVAIN: We were traveling around to do those gigs. We had this big station wagon that was rented through our promoter. We're driving in Florida and Elvis Presley comes on the radio, "Heartbreak Hotel." Jerry and Johnny, they're sitting together behind me. I turned 'round and said, "*Heartbreakers*. Wouldn't that be a great name for a band?"

PETER JORDAN: The place where Jerry's mother lived was called Crystal Springs, and she had a little motor court. So we go down there and everything is good.

SYLVAIN SYLVAIN: She had a house and she had all these trailers. She was married to this guy, and they were really *his* trailers. They would rent out the trailers as hotel rooms. And we go to gigs and come back and stay. Jerry, of course, stayed in the house, but she would have dinner for us every night. Man, we'd have fried chicken and corn, mashed potatoes…. Finally, we were eating again! Arthur's there with us. Frenchie didn't come. He stayed up in the loft on 23rd Street, which was a big mistake, because Frenchie really took care of us, and he had a way of slowing down David's and everybody's ego. We all wanted to work. We were all trying to make it work. Including David.

PETER JORDAN: We all knew that both Johnny and Jerry were strung out. First couple of days are going good. There's a kid down there named Jim Marshall—and he has documented this himself, so I'm not outing him — he and his friends happen to be Dolls fans, and they came to see the shows, And conversing with Johnny and Jerry, they mention they wanted to cop. They had a friend who knew where to cop. All right. So the guy would go to fucking Tampa, wherever the hell it was. We're in a little resort town. Everything was going swell. The kid got busted. He got busted, and went to jail copping—obviously he had his own problems. All of a sudden, they had no dope. So a day goes by, two days go by—who knows what it is. And they are getting more and more antsy.

SYLVAIN SYLVAIN: It's very hard for anybody to score, especially back in 1975 in Tampa, Florida.

PETER JORDAN: Now this motor court was six little trailers that looked like crickets around a house, and it looked like the house by Bates Motel. That's where Jerry's mother and stepfather lived. So we're in these little trailers. Now Arthur is decompressing and decomposing, and I'm supposed to live with him. And there's no air conditioning. And it's summer time. So he smells like shit—like, when alcohol's working its way out of your system. [So] I'm staying at someone else's house, and everybody else is two-on-two in a trailer.

They have an argument at dinner. Johnny and Jerry's personal opinion as they were presenting it, was that this is not going to work—we cannot tour the South and work our way to California. (Which is a valid idea, I might add.) We have to go back to New York and make peace with Leber-Krebs and start from scratch there. Get back with our old management, [even if it's] a little disingenuous on both sides. They wanted to get back to New York—pronto.

They didn't want to compromise, and David told them, "Everyone's replaceable." And they said, "Fuck you," and left. And [they] went straight back to New York and started The Heartbreakers, which are obviously advertising for clean living.

You know, there's no doubt in anyone's mind that they indeed were strung out. It wasn't just a nasty rumor made to make them look bad.

SYLVAIN SYLVAIN: David…you can't confront him, even if it's good advice. And he'd been drinking way, way too much since 1973. Every day, like wake up in the morning and *bam*. And it's whisky and gin, not just a beer or two, you know. He did it all the way through his Buster Poindexter days, where he's famous for having a martini, and that became his show. It certainly never hurt his voice. He's always had that gorgeous raspy, bluesy man's voice. But as we were sitting down and eating one night—and yeah, Jerry Nolan and Johnny Thunders, they've got monkeys on their backs (as Malcolm McLaren used to describe it), and they're itching, but they're trying to make it work; they're there to make it work. [David] got really,

really nasty with us. This was not the first time, but this was the last time. He just basically said, at the end of the whole conversation, that we were all replaceable. And not that it *was* his show, but it was going to *be* his show. We were in shock that he's even saying this to us, because you can't really replace the Dolls.

NINA ANTONIA: They're all exhausted, they're all strung out, hung-over.... And it must have been terrible in red patent leather.

SYLVAIN SYLVAIN: The last words that I heard from Jerry—and I would have probably said the same thing myself—were when I was driving him to the airport with Johnny and Malcolm McLaren. They got out, and were walking towards the entrance of the airport. I yelled out loud, "Hey, you guys! What about the New York Dolls?" Johnny kept on walking, but Jerry turned around. He said, "Fuck the New York Dolls." I swear to god. I don't mean to make him look mean, or nasty, or [like] a junkie or anything else. I would have said the same fucking thing. We were all trying to keep it going, and David was the last straw, so mean and so cold. It wasn't just that he said it to Johnny and Jerry. He said it to me, too, when he said, "You're *all* replaceable." What does "all" mean? It only means one thing: You're *all* replaceable.

NINA ANTONIA: You know, things were not going good. But I think for somebody like Jerry, who was a very principled man (and for Jerry and Johnny, who gave everything that they could to the New York Dolls)…I don't think he could take hearing something like that. No. I've heard other stories about drugs, and this and that, but I think probably being told that *anybody* could be replaced is a pretty hard thing to swallow. So….

SYLVAIN SYLVAIN: They go back home. And then Malcolm came up to me and said, "Mate, we're broke. We need some money, so let's take a few shows"—shows that we already had booked. So I went up to Arthur, who was hanging round with these [local] guys. I asked Arthur, "Do these guys play music?" And he said, "Yeah, yeah, yeah. This guy plays guitar and the other one plays the drums." I said, "This is pretty fucking cool." So I teased up the guy's hair and I put him in the back a little bit. This guy turns out to be Blackie Lawless and his drummer at the time; I don't know what his name was. But we did, like, one or two shows and that was it. That was *it*.

PETER JORDAN: Blackie Gooseman's been hanging around all week. That's his last name: Blackie Gooseman. He lived down there. He's from Queens. He used to know Ace Frehley when they went to the fucking kindergarten together. So we got these two nights at a club. He learns the songs. He did two shows. That was his involvement in the Dolls; that was it. Arthur inherits most of the amps, which are left in Blackie Gooseman's mother's garage. He and Arthur go to California. Sylvain and Malcolm take a trip to New Orleans, a sightseeing trip, where Malcolm gets the clap. David goes back to New York. I hang around long enough to dispose of some of the paperwork, and I hitchhike back to the city. And that's it. That was the end of the Dolls.

SYLVAIN SYLVAIN: Then, David goes back to New York. Now we have a little money, so we flew David back to New York. Me and Malcolm we have the station wagon. I said to Malcolm, "Hey, have you ever been to New Orleans?" And he said, "No, mate, never been. I always wanted to go. My favorite band, Professor Longhair, blah blah blah." I said, "Let's go." We drove to New Orleans. I didn't even have a license, by the way, but I drove. I actually convinced him to take me to the Louisiana Motor Vehicle Department to pass my test, and I *did* pass my test. And he, you know, tested me outside of the place: "Alright, mate, what do you do? You come to a stop light, what do you do?" I said, "You fuckin' stop." And I pass my test. I get my permit—temporary license, but at least I have a license to drive back to New York. Arthur Kane stays in Florida with Blackie Lawless, and they start playing together and all this. And actually Blackie Lawless was a fucking jewel, because years and years later…Arthur once told me that he was really broke, and one day, you know, [after] Blackie Lawless became a huge fucking star, he never forgot that, and he once got in touch with Arthur Kane and sent him like, $15,000. So that's pretty solid. I like this guy! Although they got my amp. I had this beautiful old Fender cream-color Tremaluxe, and I left it down there with Arthur to take care of it, and he gave it to Blackie. I don't know what the fuck *he* did with it. But anyway….

WALTER LURE: I learned later on that Jerry and Johnny hated David all along because, you know, it was like "Personality Crisis": David wanted to run the band his way. I don't want to say anything bad about him, but David was more of a socialite and an entertainment guy, whereas Johnny and Jerry are more rock 'n' roll, blues, down-to-earth guys. They didn't like the fact that David brought in Todd Rundgren. Johnny and Jerry were always complaining if they didn't get their way as well—as I'm sure David would do if he didn't get [his way], so…the seeds were already there for them to break up. The Red Patent tour was just sort of boring, you know? It was like, staged. They all had the same clothes on. It was almost like putting on a revival rock show or something like that, Beatles suits. It just didn't work for the Dolls. It didn't have any rawness.

NITE BOB: When you're an innovator, it's really hard. You're chopping a path through the jungle. 20 years later, 30 years later, culture catches up with you. You don't make no money. You just cut a path for other people and then lesser, less outrageous bands will [be successful].

Oh yeah, I'll admit we used to look at Aerosmith as kind of like a cheesy, Boston version of the Dolls. But that's kind of harsh, too, because they…that was the look at that time period. You're in a band you want to have the current look that's happening. Be it spandex, be it goofy hats, whatever. Platform shoes…the shoes were pretty funny, too.

MARTY THAU: They self-destructed. They imploded, but they left a trail of influence that others picked up on and ran with, and were reasonably successful too. I mean, The Clash, Sex Pistols….

LENNY KAYE: They predicted not only the coming of punk, but the renaissance of garage rock, the sense of getting back to basics. That is a theme throughout rock 'n' roll history, whether it's Nirvana or the White Stripes… the sense of returning to the root of why you do it in the first place. To turn it up, to have those three chords circulating and to howl at the top of your lungs. That's really what it's about, and the Dolls predicted that future by returning the music to its sense of why it began in the first place.

WALTER LURE: The Dolls were a breath of fresh air. They were basic rock 'n' roll, the shortest songs you could think of. They were like the Ramones before the Ramones. Simple songs, good songs. They did great covers of '50s and '60s songs. If Johnny or Arthur Kane could pick up a guitar and learn how to play in two weeks, than anyone could do it, so it sort of opened the window to say, "I love this music and I can do it like anyone else." That's what the Dolls represented. They brought rock back to the basics and it opened, and it started a whole scene. And it really started a worldwide scene, in a sense, because of punk. It might have come about, who knows? But it really started with the Dolls, and then after that Television and the Ramones. They were children of the Dolls.

Sylvain Sylvain: I'm the biggest New York Dolls fan that there ever was. *I love the New York Dolls.* I want people to know that. That the reason why I did it again is just to do it like the New York Dolls—although I thought that's not what really projected in the second wave, you know. I just wanted to keep Johnny's name alive. Jerry Nolan's name. Arthur Kane. Poor Billy Murcia and the whole…what we had invented back then. And I want people to always know that. Man, you know, everything that I've done is just to keep, you know, the *love* that we all had together, to keep it going. There's nothing else.

Born to Lose

LEEE BLACK CHILDERS: New York has the streets. It's all there are. There are little pocket parts and there's Central Park, but basically you're living on the streets when you're in New York.

It just got crazier and crazier, until by the end of the '70s, all of us who lived through it—and a lot of us didn't live through it—think it's the most fabulous age there ever was. It was like Greece or Rome. It was all the creativity that could have been shoved into a tiny, sweaty, dangerous, dark little pocket of humanity, all there at once.

There was disco, which a lot of people hated. Now when you look back on it, what's to hate? It was pretty cool, actually. There was punk, of course. Then there were those crazy black kids who would plug their turn-tables into municipal light poles and start scratching. All happening at the same time and all killing each other at the same time and all hating each other at the same time and yet, all intermingling....

Times Square was a ghost land, even the rent boys and the prostitutes were afraid of it by that time. If you went to Times Square, all the marquees on the old theaters had weird signs on them saying THE END HAS COME. It was dark and crazy, and you couldn't walk down the street without getting mugged. There was a garbage strike, so all the garbage piled up to about the third floor, and then people set fire to it. So the city was literally in flames. Son of Sam was killing people. It was the ideal city. It was perfect. It was great. The greatest rock 'n' roll there could possibly be.

If you were at Max's Kansas City and you needed to go just a short distance down to CBGB's, at least eight people would go together because it was too dangerous even to go that little space.

It was the most fabulous time that could have ever been. It was dangerous, it was crazy, you could get robbed, murdered, burnt up, burgled, raped, all those things! And you knew it and you loved it.

And yet the greatest music…all the greatest music that could be possibly be born was being born, because of the danger and because of the craziness.

RICHARD LLOYD: On the lower East Side, rampant heroin and cocaine sales were taking place. You could go to a certain block and see a line down the street and around the corner that looked like the line to go to a hit movie. There's these Puerto Rican kids walking up and down saying, "No singles. Decide what you want. Put your money in the hole. Your bags will come out the bottom of the door." There were lawyers with their briefcases and you know, it was a bizarre thing. We all got strung out.

BOB GRUEN: I once discussed with Johnny about how hard it is to be a junkie. It's not easy because first of all, you don't buy heroin in a delicatessen or luncheonette (actually, some you do), but you have to find them. It's illegal. It's hard to find. It's hard to find good quality. Because it's illegal, there's no regulations. You're dealing with other people who are drugged out of their mind. There's a lot of danger involved. You're going into really bad neighborhoods at really bad hours of the day and night, and what I talked about with Johnny was that, when you're talking drugs, you can't call in sick. It's a full-time, 24-hour job, because you only get enough to go for a little while.

When you're actually addicted to the drugs, if you run out, you get very, very sick; so sick, that you can't do anything. You *need* those drugs to be able to function in any way at all, and so taking the drugs becomes your first obligation. Anything else—a band, a girlfriend, an apartment—any other thing in your life becomes second to getting the drugs.

MARCIA RESNICK: It coincided with the amount of drugs that were available in the neighborhood. There were drugs on every street corner being sold and the availability was so tremendous. And the angst—the level of angst in New York City—was pretty tremendous also. [Back] then, you could live very cheaply in New York. So everybody lived in the cheap neighborhoods, the cheapest neighborhoods, and it was drug time. What can I say? Everybody was experimenting and getting hooked. The quality of the drugs was really good at that time, depending on your tolerance.

Johnny had a pretty high tolerance. He needed a lot of drugs. I had a very low tolerance. I don't recall Johnny ever trying to get off drugs during those days. Everybody was just on drugs and took it for granted.

FRANK INFANTE: The Lower East Side back then…you just went there to cop heroin. There was no other reason for me to be there, or Johnny or anybody else. The rents were cheap and all, but there was no point in going there unless you were going to get drugs. You had a place like CBGB's, anybody could go down there and get a gig and play without going through the rigmarole. Basically it was taken over by a certain bunch of people, certain bands.

PHYLLIS STEIN: The whole scene really was concentrated in Max's and CBGB's. Some bands were Max's bands, some bands were CBGB's bands, and sometimes there was crossover. The Dolls had been a Max's band, so it was a natural progression for The Heartbreakers to do that and be a Max's band.

DONNA DESTRI: There was like an unwritten rule: If you played at CBGB's, you had to wait a month and *then* you can play at Max's, [and] vice-versa. Hilly and Tommy Dean always had a little rivalry going.

ANDY SHERNOFF: Nobody wanted to go to the Bowery. No record company wanted to go down there. So what would happen is, Dictators would play one week—we'd play Thursday, Friday, Saturday. Two shows a night, six shows a weekend. Then the next weekend, Television would do that. Then the weekend after that, The Heartbreakers, then the Ramones, then Blondie, and then we would do it again. It was a great training ground, because nobody cared. No music business cared.

Audience was very small. The CBGB's stage was close to the front. People think of it how it was in the back, but there was a pool table back there. You're getting maybe 100, 150 people in the early days. New York City at the time was falling apart. You can get cheap rent. You can get rent for $150 a month, $200 a month, so you could work a few days in the month, pay your bills, and spend the rest of the time being a musician. *Now*, to get an apartment in New York, you're spending thousands of dollars. You can't be an artist in New York. For artists to breed and create, you need cheap rent, because it's not always a money making experience.

A few factors fell into place to allow that whole scene to happen, and one of them was, New York was a hell-hole. Drugs on the street. City was bankrupt, and artists moved into cheap-rent apartments, and that helped the scene evolve. It wasn't just musicians; there were filmmakers, poets, writers…and they all would go to the shows, and a lot of people in the audience are well known in their field.

MARCIA RESNICK: It was electric. It was exciting to be there. My friends were there. But what I really liked to do was bring people who never went there before and didn't belong there and see what happened. There was a big mix of people there. Norman Mailer was there once.

I brought Ron Kovic around the time that they were thinking of making the book of *Born on the Fourth of July* into a movie. He was talking to a peace march, and then he came to CBGB's in his wheelchair. We were seeing The Contortions and he was stunned, exhilarated by this. Before that, I only saw him exhilarated when he talked about war.

SYLVAIN SYLVAIN: Once we finally made it to New York, we were selling some of Malcolm's clothes. All the time, he said to me, "Mate, what do you want to do? My wife's got all these kids hanging around the shop and we could put a great band together for you." "All right. Well, let's try it, you know." And he said to me, "Look, give me your guitar and your piano." I had a Fender Rhodes piano that you could hear on *Red Patent Leather*, kind of sounds a little jazzy. It's not really my kind of piano, but at the time that's the only thing you could buy for a couple of hundred bucks that was a keyboard, electric. And he said, "Give me your guitar," which was a white Les Paul with a decal of a girl on it.

This is the guitar [I played], by the way, after the airlines had broken the neck of the Gretsch Falcon. That brought me to tears, and the guys said "Don't worry," especially Johnny. Johnny had a heart. He said, "Man, don't worry, you'll get another one." Couldn't find a Gretsch, but I bought that Les Paul at Manny's Music, on 48th Street. We probably still owe them money.

So what happened was, Malcolm said to me, "Give me your guitar and I'll send you a plane ticket." Now, he did send me, like, a letter. A seven-page letter that's hanging up now at the Rock and Roll Hall of Fame, and it goes for seven pages, man. It says, on the back of the letter: "Mrs. Mizrahi, please give this letter to your son—URGENT. A Friend From England."

Inside, man, it's like these little quarter-booth photos: "This guy, he can't sing, but he can definitely sing better than David Johansen." Turns out to be pictures of Johnny Rotten and Steve Jones. He's wearing a real like, English cap and they don't look nothing like the Sex Pistols. "And they're great! They're going to be your band, Sylvain. Come to England! I don't trust this one and I don't trust that one."

To make a long story short, I'm still waiting for that fucking plane ticket.

BOB GRUEN: Johnny called me up and asked me if I would come by and take pictures. He and Jerry and Richard Hell were forming a band together and they called it The Heartbreakers, and I did a series of pictures. I went and met them on 23rd Street, in the Piano Building. They were rehearsing. We took some pictures on the fire escape out back. We came down here and took some pictures out on the waterfront, and they actually played a few shows.

WALTER LURE: I joined a band in Brooklyn. Mark Bell's brother was in it, the guitar player, Fred Bell. I met this other guitar player, Marty, who knew this singer, Eliot [Kidd], from The Demons; The Demons were starting. This is like '74 or something.

Since Eliot was the singer of The Demons—and he knew the Dolls cause he used to deal drugs or something like that, whatever his line of business was—we would share the rehearsal loft. The Dolls would also use the loft, but they were away.

The Demons were getting ready to do their first show, and word had come round that the Dolls had broken up; so they weren't going to be rehearsing there anymore. It was a shame, but after seeing their *Red Patent Leather* shows, we knew it was the beginning of the end, in spite of Malcolm and his machinations.

[So] The Demons did their first show, and there were rumors that Johnny and Jerry had teamed up with Richard Hell. But I didn't know that they were looking for another guitar player.

NINA ANTONIA: So Johnny and Jerry come back from Florida and they recruit Richard Hell, who has this great stripped-down look and he's got a name for himself as a poet. He was in Television.

WALTER LURE: The Demons played our first show at the 82 Club, and Johnny showed up with Jerry. After the show was over, Johnny pulls me on the side and says, "Don't tell Eliot this, but would you like to join our band?" I'm going, "Yeah, yeah. Tell me about it."

He set up for me to come to an audition a couple of weeks later. It was him and Hell and Jerry in the studio in midtown, 28th Street, I think. And I played, and then I didn't hear from him for a couple of months.

Then The Demons had an opening gig with The Heartbreakers out in Queens, in this place called Coventry. After the show, Jerry said, "Well, did you like anything about the band at all?" I'm going, "Yeah, yeah. I love the songs." So they said, "You wanna join the band?" So that was it, I'm in the band.

LENNY KAYE: I really loved The Heartbreakers. I liked it when Richard and Johnny joined forces, because Richard is a wild card at best, and Johnny has his thing. They also captured a New York sensibility—"Chinese Rocks" and that sense of dissolute abandon that probably wasn't good for any of them. They were a great rock 'n' roll band.

RICHARD LLOYD: I went to see them at Max's with Johnny and Richard Hell, and I thought they were incredible. I mean, the *drive*! It was…like a freight train, you know? But it was very different from the Dolls as well.

NINA ANTONIA: There were some people that felt that with the Dolls, Johnny and Jerry had had their moment in the spotlight, and they were the bad boys of the band and they'd somehow sabotaged the Dolls. The Heartbreakers had a real fight on their hands. Okay, they've got two former Dolls in the line-up, which is great in some aspects, but not in others. But they develop this great band that was so very different from the Dolls. It does go right back to their fifties roots. It is about rock 'n' roll purity. It stripped away what now seemed redundant about the Dolls.

WALTER LURE: Hell contributed a lot. He was more authentic of this new wave punk, where a lot of people thought Johnny and Jerry already had their chance in the Dolls, and resented the fact that they were trying to come up again through the punk scene. There was a sort of undercurrent of "these guys aren't really hip because they came from before." It took a bit of a transition period, but Hell gave it a lot of authenticity cause he had the whole "Blank Generation" thing.

MARCIA RESNICK: I loved The Heartbreakers. I loved that Johnny continued to make music after the Dolls. I had a real kinship with The Heartbreakers—for all the wrong reasons. I was using and they were using and it was sort of a family affair of people who were dependent on drugs. It wasn't only that, but the songs, the words in the songs meant something to me.

WALTER LURE: I wasn't an innocent as far as drugs were concerned. I had done smack maybe once or twice, never stuck a needle in my arm. I used to smoke a lot of pot and take speed and pills and LSD in school, but that was the standard '60s cocktail mix.

I got in the band and Johnny and Jerry and Hell were all into it, and Dee Dee Ramone would be hanging out too. He was part of it. There were places to cop on the East Side. Avenue A was a no man's land back then, so you could get stuff around there. They would get it on First Avenue, there'd be a couple of delis that would sell it.

I'd be sitting in and watching them getting off, and you had to be cool to do it. They didn't really force me to do it, but it was, of course, part and parcel of the band and the attitude: Be a beatnik, be a junkie—this cool thing. Like an idiot, I got into it. It was fun for a bit, then of course, later on it just gets out of hand.

In the beginning, the first year or so when we were rehearsing, it was no problem; you know, they would come late every now and then when they wanted to go score, but they would show. Rehearsed twice a week, which is amazing. Later on, we'd be lucky if we rehearsed once a year.

It didn't turn that way overnight. Jerry thought it was cool 'cause he was with that whole fifties *Man With the Golden Arm, Hatful of Rain* movie stuff. It had that whole mystique of being like the underside of society, the outcast—with good reason. Johnny was, you know, cool like Jerry. That was the mentality, and they didn't get away from it.

LEEE BLACK CHILDERS: I went to CBGB's, and there were The Heart-breakers with Richard Hell, who I loved. He didn't have any idea how he looked; he just really looked scary and dangerous. That's when I realized, *there's a whole new world happening here.* And guess what? I liked the other one.

I liked this world, too, of chapped lips and purple eyes and craziness. I knew there was a lot of drugs involved, but heaven knows, I've been through enough drugs with the previous rock 'n' roll world I'd been involved in, so it didn't bother me at all. The Heartbreakers were Richard Hell and Johnny Thunders and Walter Lure and Jerry Nolan. You can't get more drug saturated than that and, but there's a big thing between Richard Hell and Johnny Thunders. There always is in all bands: Who are *they*—the little girls—looking at?

I'd stopped working for MainMan; my idea was just to be a photographer, and go down and photograph the bands at CBGB's. I loved the Ramones, I loved Blondie; they were obviously going to take off. I was working for *Rock Scene* magazine, *Hit Parader*…so I had a job. I was OK.

One night at CBGB's, the conflict between Richard Hell and Johnny Thunders had come to a final, complete thing. Both of them were stars, and neither one of them knew they were stars. Mick Jagger didn't know he was a star; that's what caused the problem with Brian Jones. Then in the Dolls, it was David Johansen and Johnny Thunders. Johnny didn't know that he was as much a star as David was, so then there was a problem. Then what's he do? He gets Richard Hell, the biggest ego in the world, in the band with him! Only Richard didn't know—*really* know—he was a star either. And so it's a whole thing also about "What are we going to do? We just must hate each other." And so they did. Do you know the famous story about Alain Delon and Jean-Paul…what was his name? Belmondo! They did a movie together, they actually had in their contract the number of close-ups each one of them could have and it had to be exactly equal. Well, it got to be that with Johnny Thunders and Richard Hell. The same number of guitar moments, the same number of vocal moments. It's crazy, you can't run a band like that!

Richard Hell just said, "I'm out of here." So he was gone, and he was gone that night—*gone*. Bang! In front of us. And that's how they do it. I've seen so many bands break up on stage. He just walked off and he was gone.

I was standing there with Tony Zanetta, who was the president of Main-Man. And we had done David Bowie together…so much together. We had schemed everything together and done everything together. And we went, "Oh my god."

And at that moment, Johnny Thunders walks up. (And you know, he was not the tallest person on earth, anyway; he was like a Tom Cruise kinda guy.) And he walked up to us and said, "Well, the band broke up. I'm going to have to get a new bass player. We want to go on. Do you want to manage us?"

I'd never thought of myself as a manager at all! And I looked at Tony Zanetta and I said, "What do you say? Let's manage 'em."

Tony Zanetta said, "Are you crazy? They're junkies. They're nuts. They're totally uncontrollable. Do you think David Bowie was impossible? How far down do you want to drag yourself into the seventh circle of hell? This is the worst idea you've ever had in your life. No. Don't do this."

And I went, "I'm gonna do it." So Tony didn't do it and I did. It's the greatest decision I ever made.

PHYLLIS STEIN: Johnny and Jerry decided that they were going to ask [Richard] to leave the band. They were down in Sunset Studios, which is where they always rehearsed, and he walked in and he was going to quit the band. It kind of happened at the same time. The way Jerry told me, he thought Richard was just going to come in and take over. He wanted to do his songs, and Johnny and Jerry looked at him like, "What's he, nuts?" You know. So that was the end of him.

WALTER LURE: He was like another version of David, where he wanted to run everything. He was telling Johnny, like, "You can only sing two songs in the set, and Walter can sing one song every three gigs" or something like that. Johnny just said, "Fuck you," and walked out. This is after we'd been playing together for maybe a year or so. It was like, we rehearsed for a while and we did a few gigs which were good…but then Hell just started trying to take more and more. He had this vision of himself as some dissolute French poet giving his message out to the world through rock 'n' roll. Johnny walked out, and we ended up following him.

BILLY RATH: Richard Hell wrote great songs, but it wasn't quite the same.

He was more punk actually. You know he had that political poetry stuff in his life. Great guy. "Blank Generation." Incredible.

NINA ANTONIA: I'm gonna break out of history and tell you my Richard Hell story. I went to interview him, and um, he was pretty pissed that I'd taken Johnny's side in the story. He was talking to me about Johnny's lyrics, and he was saying how could I like a song when the lyrics are "baby I love you, I really do." He said that he was so mad at me, he was going to hang me from outside the hotel window. (He didn't.)

It should have been a great marriage, Hell and The Heartbreakers. But I think [Hell] tried to galvanize the band, and Jerry Nolan wasn't having any of it. So then they got in Billy Rath.

BILLY RATH: When I first started playing with The Heartbreakers, I was unknown in the city, and it was just a perfect match. I was a rocker from way back. I grew up with that sound, the '60s and the '50s, and that was my style.

Always a bass player, never a guitar player. In fact, [I got] my first bass [when] my sister gave me her guitar. She had an electric guitar and I pulled two strings off it, made it a bass guitar. So I think that made a big difference and everybody in New York was, "Who's this guy? Who's this guy?"

We played Max's and the house was just packed. It was just really hot. You know everybody was dying to see what The Heartbreakers—what Johnny—was all about, because there was no tension now. Richard Hell was a poet and Johnny was a rock 'n' roller, and so that caused a little tension.

WALTER LURE: Billy had been living in Miami and floating around from band to band. Billy was a weird guy. He was quiet and didn't really say much, but he was a great bass player. He just had a natural feel for bass. So he fit right in, as soon as we had the audition. It was over on East 10th Street, somewhere on Avenue D. We had tried a few different bass players and Billy just stood out. He was a natural. We didn't know his personality, but it was like, we didn't really care. It just didn't matter. He wanted to join the band! As far as I know, he wasn't a junkie, so that was a plus—though

PHOTO: PHYLLIS STEIN

that didn't last very long.

He also wasn't a star or an egomaniac where you didn't have to deal with a Richard Hell or one of these personalities. We didn't really need ideas out of him, 'cause the three of us had enough ideas on our own. So it was actually good, in a sense. He was a stand-up guy who you could depend on, like a foundation. You didn't have to worry about him trying to change this or that. He did give us a different level.

Some people didn't really like the fact that we didn't have that beatnik fringe look anymore, with Hell. But it didn't really make a difference, cause we were never about that side of punk anyway—apart from the drug side of it. We were a rock band that happened to come out in the middle of the punk scene, so we took advantage of it. We ripped up a few of our clothes, but to us, it was always rock music.

BILLY RATH: I grew up in Boston, so I was the odd man out in the band. Growing-up-wise, my scene was different than Johnny and Jerry's, and of course Walter was an intellectual. Walter always read; he'd go to museums and stuff. But you're right about Jerry and Johnny. Johnny looked up to Jerry, and what Jerry would say, Johnny basically went along with. So it was good. But I was the odd man out. I could feel it sometimes; never from Johnny, only from Jerry. Walter never made me feel that way. And Johnny never made me feel that way. The only one who would was Jerry, unfortunately. We played well together. It was just was because I wasn't a New Yawker.

JOHN PERRY: The Heartbreakers clearly were drawing on '50s rock. Short, punchy songs. Lots of attack. Very visual. Everything up front. And the simplicity of '50s rock too.

BILLY RATH: The Heartbreakers had soul. Heart. And we were influenced by Eddie Cochran and all the bands in the '50s; Elvis…and then of course putting the edge on it. The Dolls were a big influence, because of Johnny and Jerry. But when The Heartbreakers came out it, was a new sound. It was the rock 'n' roll band that they had been looking for.

WALTER LURE: Jerry would write, like, "Take a Chance," "Can't Keep My Eyes on You"…. He had written most of the song, and he had the chorus, but he just didn't like writing words. So he asked me, "Here, you wanna write the words?" 'Cause he liked a lotta the words I wrote. So I said, "OK." And then he said, "Oh we'll be a songwriting team"—like Lennon/McCartney or Jagger/Richards or something like that. And so I said, "OK, we'll put our names on the song." You know, none of us were making zillions of dollars at the time, so it didn't really make a difference. You can probably sort of tell which songs are mine and which songs are his. But "One Track Mind" was all mine, and "Can't Keep" and "Take a Chance" were mostly his. I would put an extra verse or two cause the music was already written.

"All By Myself" was the one that we actually wrote together, because we were playing a beat and I started playing some chords and then he came up with a chorus and I started with the lyrics. That was the one that was actually was done in tandem. The other ones were sort of pieces that we just put each other's names on.

BOB GRUEN: That band basically revolved around drugs – not as a band, but as individual members. I don't think Walter got too much into it. I think Billy did. But certainly Johnny and Jerry were pretty deeply involved with heroin at that point.

BILLY RATH: When I joined The Heartbreakers, I was straight at the beginning, and it makes a big difference. To me, that's the best high you can get: To go on stage and play, without any kind of drug influence in your system. You feel the energy from each player.

Johnny had so much energy. You know, he'd come over and he'd play in front. I'd be back here with Jerry. He'd come in front, and smile and wink and do his twists, and spin around and push me around a little bit. He liked to do that. He liked to push us around. It was all part of the act. I mean, he wasn't pushing hard; it was part of the act. We were bad boys, you know? And that's the image that was projected.

WALTER LURE: Leee came on after Hell left. Leee knew Johnny and Jerry from the Dolls phase. It just sounded good, because we really needed a manager. We needed somebody who could get gigs, take care of business...'cause none of us were capable of doing that, at that point.

Anarchy

LEEE BLACK CHILDERS: It was hard. But we had three years of the greatest rock 'n' roll—the most historic rock 'n' roll—that could have possibly been produced. Because it lead to the next three years, which no one could have predicted. Malcolm McLaren didn't know. No one knew what was going to happen over the next three years.

In December of 1976, we were on the road with the Sex Pistols and The Clash and The Damned, doing the Anarchy tour. I'd never heard of any of them before, as you know. All music…fashion…*everything* changed! And it wasn't planned, not even Malcolm McLaren, bless his heart and rest his soul, not even *he* knew what he'd gotten himself into. We were in way over our heads, and there it was. Suddenly it was punk rock and it was in the media. Media went crazy, and we just had to deal with it. And we did good. We changed the world.

BILLY RATH: We got an invite to go to England on the Sex Pistols' tour, which was a great opening for us. Now the Sex Pistols messed it up when they went on TV—all the gigs got canceled. Jerry and Johnny and Walter and myself in one room with bunk beds, living on fifty pence a day, with a light bulb hanging down from the ceiling with no shade at all. It was very interesting. We had to figure out: Are we going to buy cigarettes? Are we going to buy bread? Are we going to spend it on something else?

NINA ANTONIA: The Heartbreakers touched down on December 1st 1976, the same day that the Sex Pistols are on the [Bill Grundy] *Today* show. And there's a bit of a national scandal brewing, because they swear on the Bill Grundy show. So they're supposed to do the Anarchy tour with the Pistols and The Damned. Loads of those shows were pulled because of fear about people's morals.

BILLY RATH: We landed and all of a sudden this whole thing is plastered all over the papers about the Pistols and how bad it was. But they were young kids, just learning how to play, and we were seasoned musicians. We had been playing, we were a couple of years older, we had experience, and the band was magic, too. It was a hand in the glove. To play in that band was so wonderful. I can't really describe it. It was spiritual, as I said. Energy-wise, the emotion was there. The fun was there. Like driving down the street in a '57 Chevy with a convertible top, a nice blue-eyed blonde ponytail girl sitting beside you, maybe heading to a drive-in theater.... I mean, that's what we were all about.

WALTER LURE: Well, it just amazed the shit out of us that someone says "fuck" on TV. I mean, it didn't happen that much in the States, but it would sneak out every now and then. But people didn't start revolutions over it! Here in the UK, every newspaper had these blaring headlines.... Horrible fucking thing. They all curse like anyone else, but there were people kicking their televisions and complaining. It started this whole controversy that spread through the whole country like wildfire. Britain is like that. Fads can start real quick, cause it's a small country.

We landed, we didn't know what was going on. Malcolm was white. He picked us up in a limo, but he was going, "Uh huh, I don't know what's going on. We don't know what's happening with the tour now." Because of all this controversy. For days, it was like, a headline on all the tabloids. Johnny would be going, "So, someone said 'fuck' on TV. Someone says 'fuck' all over the place!" But it turned out really big, and it was the best thing that could have happened, because they got ten times more publicity with it. It wasn't great for the tour, 'cause we had like, twenty-three shows or twenty-six shows, and we ended up playing six of them, cause they would cancel them as we would get into town. We would end up sitting in the hotel bar at night, getting drunk with The Clash and the Pistols and all, so.... But that's how we got to be friends, so that was good in that way.

BILLY RATH: At the beginning when we went on that Sex Pistols tour, it was their tour. [Amid the controversy,] we were offered all the gigs [ourselves]. The venues said that we could go and do them. And of course that would've put money in our pockets, kept us living. But it was the Sex Pistols' tour, and we're rock 'n' rollers, and we honor other rock 'n' rollers, you know? It was *their* show. So we said no, and we did go out and get our own gig and played by ourselves. But as far as the tour goes, we only did what the Pistols were allowed to play.

There was one date we played in Cardiff, it was funny. Johnny and I were laughing so much. We drive up and there's these people picketing "the Devil's music." There was a preacher across the street with a PA system telling people not to go into the show: "It's nothing but the devil's music!" And what's really interesting is, years later he apologized for doing that! That was about ten years later. The preacher actually apologized to us for being such a jerk, not appreciating the rock 'n' roll. It was far from the Devil's music. The Heartbreakers were always rock 'n' roll. We could play in front of any crowd. The rockers liked us. The skinheads liked us. The punkers loved us.

TERRY CHIMES: The Clash did that Anarchy tour with them. I didn't do that tour. I'd left the band at that point, so I never saw them. So they were talking all excited about this band, and "Oh, they're really good." They really liked the band. But I think a lot of bands were threatened by The Heartbreakers, 'cause they were so good.

BILLY RATH: When we went on that tour with the Pistols, they were good but they weren't great. They were learning. They were little London boys who were learning how to play, learning how to do the stage thing. Of course they did it well; I'm not putting down The Clash and the Pistols.

The Damned walked out on us. We were originally the opening band, and The Clash came on after us, and The Damned, and the Pistols. And we felt bad for them, because we came out and we could play. And they were just learning how to play. So immediately they shifted us to just before The Pistols, and The Damned got all uptight. They didn't feel that was right.

NINA ANTONIA: Leee was getting quite desperate. They were living in Splendor, at Sebastian Conran's house. I believe it was Joe Strummer that told The Heartbreakers or Leee that there was this lovely mansion where they could stay rent free. So Leee had a roof over their heads, but things like food were quite hard for them to come by. The first really important show that they do was at the Roxy in Covent Garden, which only had a capacity of 150, but that was really…. With the Anarchy tour falling apart, the Roxy show really put The Heartbreakers on the map. They apparently absolutely rocked the joint. Johnny and Jerry came to London as sort of low-life royalty, you know?

WALTER LURE: They didn't have the resentment that they had over here; they were idols over there. The night we landed, Malcolm decided to take us all out to dinner. Rotten showed up later, but Steve Jones and Paul Cook came to meet us at the hotel with Malcolm and their assistant. He's real quiet, standing in the corner, and we said, "Hello," you know. Later, I heard that they were in awe of Johnny and Jerry, because they were from the Dolls and they were their heroes. I didn't realize the influence of the Dolls over there, as opposed to some of the other groups.

JOHN PERRY: Punk's starting up, although it's a fairly small thing in London. Probably less than a hundred people, and their background is probably more art school than professional musician. And into this suddenly come The Heartbreakers, with a background in R'n'B, who can really play. The Pistols weren't a bad band, but exempting the Pistols…. Most of the bands of that era, at that point, couldn't play very well, and they certainly didn't know about much about playing *together*. The Heartbreakers had Nolan who's a lovely drummer, they know how to play together.

Yeah, The Heartbreakers. It was like putting a heavyweight in amongst a bunch of kids. It was a thing to see. The Heartbreakers came over and they're plunged into Malcolm's scene, where there's people who they like, but musically, aren't their grade. John was pleased to meet The Only Ones,. He was saying they were his favorite band, musicians that knew what they were doing.

PETER PERRETT: Lots of English punk bands were more for the image, the laugh. There were lots of people who couldn't play their instruments, and it was fun having the nerve to go onstage and make a racket. And that's what most people were getting off on, something so comical. That's what

Walter Lure, Johnny, Jerry Nolan

Photo: Phyllis Stein

the Pistols were like when I saw them in 1975; they were the funniest thing I'd seen. There was entertainment value from lots of people who couldn't play. Whereas Johnny was in the classic style of a rock band, and so it was exciting from the musical point of view, not just the visual, conceptual point of view, which is what punk was when it first happened. It was more of a concept than anything valid musically.

BILLY RATH: Punk rock…it did influence us, in some of our songs. Definitely. Being on that scene, it was an exciting time. It was the birth of something new, and to be part of that was so amazing. You know the dress, the look, the sound. True punk rock is political. It's not just this hardcore stuff that you heard American bands copying, because American bands aren't political. America…the kids are different. We grew up with so much, and the London kids didn't. You know, politics was a big part of their life, but we influenced the scene also.

NINA ANTONIA: The whole band had this sort of *Mean Streets* thing going on, plus they could play their instruments—which was quite a rarity at the time. It was like, oh my god, they could start and finish a song at the same time!

WALTER LURE: We'd been around longer. We're all a little older, which we wouldn't admit to at the time. We were like, four or five years older than the average British band. We all knew how to play a little bit better, but the British had this whole scene going, which we had *no idea* of until we got there.

To me, they were hilarious. They used to do all these nutty things on stage. The New York punks were worried about being cool, so it wasn't like the *antics* that you would get in Britain. There's good and bad things to be said about both sides, but to me, the British were so funny, I just couldn't stop laughing. I'd see bands like Eater on stage…I was laughing the whole night long, even though I couldn't understand a word they fucking sang or played or anything like that. But it was hilarious, and it was great for art and for music. Billy Idol was singing great songs with Generation X, and the Pistols were great. There was a lot more fun in the British scene than in the New York scene, even though I was part of both of them.

BILLY RATH: We had the energy of a punk band, but we aren't punk. We're rock 'n' roll. New York street rock 'n' roll with a '50s heart and 20th century cut. New York street edge. And I think that really sums up what The Heartbreakers were. What Johnny was. I believe The Heartbreakers is what the Dolls were trying to achieve, but couldn't for some reason. They just didn't get to that part. I loved the Dolls, and they were good rock 'n' roll. But it wasn't the rock 'n' roll like The Heartbreakers had. The Heartbreakers were real rock 'n' roll, and you don't see that any more.

PHYLLIS STEIN: The other thing about London that was interesting was, the audiences in London were way different than in New York. In New York, everybody had seen it all. Everybody was probably a bit older than they were in London as well, and no one was jumping and pushing and spitting; everybody was too cool to do that. So going to London and going to these live shows with these kids moshing and gobbing and…I stayed in the dressing room.

BILLY RATH: We would travel. We'd all have our own rooms, and we'd watch out for each other; tried to keep everybody on an even keel. We would all watch out for Johnny, because he did have a tendency sometimes to go over the edge.

BARRY JONES: The whole drug scene was very destructive and non-productive and inescapable in some ways. It was everywhere, once you'd crossed that threshold. We looked on them as like, they knew everything because they were wise-ass New Yorkers. We looked up to them. I've said since, in an interview about Jerry, that they hadn't even done much methadone at that time. They were only a couple of years into that whole smack thing, it was only 1977. They were pretty much novices at it and were still going hell for leather, so it was very destructive.

GAIL HIGGINS: They were junkies! What can you say? And you know, when you said it to Johnny, he'd go, "Keith Richards is a junkie." And I'd say, "Johnny, Keith Richards got famous first! *Then* he became a junkie! Not the other way around." You know, like when they wanted to call their band The Junkies.

WALTER LURE: The punks were all young kids, they were still into speed and LSD. Plus they were smoking pot, so…. It would blow our minds—*Oh god, these kids are into fucking LSD over here.* We hadn't done LSD since the '60s. It was such an annoying drug. It was fun back then when you had nothing to do but lay around and stare at a wall for twelve hours. It had nothing to do with punk. Plus, you'd be spaced out on stage. To me, LSD meant California, Jefferson Airplane. So I was like, *god, this is awful.* They did a lot of speed, plus they smoked a lot of hash.

We came over and we brought our influence, which more or less came from the older bands, because Keith Richards was a major junkie. We were the bridge between the older generation and the younger generation. In England, I didn't know any of them that were doing it; we would run into people [using] every now and then. Later on, as they got to know us, you know, there'd be more who'd get into it. Probably from our influence, or just from you know, maybe by parallel. But yeah, we were definitely the ones who started things off. Supposedly Jerry was the first one to get Johnny Rotten off; I don't know, because I never knew Johnny Rotten to be into junk.

BILLY RATH: You had Billy Idol standing around watching us. Siouxsie Sioux, and of course Sid Vicious was around doing his thing. They'd take us out to eat. We'd go. They treated us well and Johnny treated them well. Unfortunately, we also influenced them—I think a little bit too much—drug-wise, and that's the only part I didn't like about our influence on the culture. American culture. The World. That drugs—heroin—was "a cool thing to do," and I thank god I'm alive. It ain't cool. Johnny would be here. Jerry would be here. I believe The Heartbreakers would be here if it wasn't for the drugs.

PHYLLIS STEIN: They were unique, but they had a big problem. And the big problem was, no one wanted to sign them and that's because of the drug issue. Maybe they could've gotten a deal with Sire—Jerry used to say that—but no one was willing to.

PETER PERRETT: I met Johnny the first time in January 1977, at The Speakeasy in London. We'd just done, I think, our second gig. And I came offstage, and he came up and introduced himself: "Hi, I'm Johnny Thunders, I love your voice." At that time, as it was only our second gig, I hadn't loads of people telling me that, so it immediately endeared him to me. We became fond friends from then onwards, you know.

He wasn't overconfident. I'm put off by arrogance, and he wasn't like that at all. He was being humble, he was telling me he thought I was great. You know, I didn't return the compliment. I didn't know Johnny, I just met him. I'd heard the name before; Malcolm had mentioned to me a couple of years before about the New York Dolls, and how they fucked up on drugs. And I couldn't see how anyone could fuck up on drugs; I thought you had to be very stupid to fuck up on drugs. So it made me slightly wary, but we had so much in common, you know? We liked the same sort of music, the same taste in clothes.

WALTER LURE: Nancy Spungen wanted to follow Jerry around; Nancy was like a groupie over here. Enough's been said about the poor girl. Nancy had money, 'cause she was a topless dancer; she used to dance in bars over in the East Village. She'd always help Johnny and Jerry out when they needed money to score dope.

Jerry had pawned his guitar before he left to get extra money. He would call up Nancy every now and then, and Nancy volunteered to get it out for him. She flew herself over, brought the guitar with her. And she shows up at our apartment, 'cause we're all living together at the time, and we go, "What the fuck is she doing here?" But it was like, Jerry got her to get the guitar out of pawn and bring it over. She's there for a couple of hours, and they kick her out of the apartment. Take the guitar, and then kick her out. So she's on her own in the middle of London. I guess she had enough money to get a hotel room or something like that. I don't remember her around that much until later on when she was with Sid, and that became another story. I guess Jerry would keep in touch with her, or even Johnny sometimes, when they needed money....

NINA ANTONIA: Nancy had been a huge New York Dolls fan, and I think she'd availed herself of David Johansen. But she had a huge crush on Jerry Nolan, and it's important to note that Nancy had written a very good piece, a very good review of The Heartbreakers for *New York Rocker*. Nancy gets this terrible rap, but when I spoke to Jerry about her, he said that he thought that she was a pretty smart girl, actually, and they were kind of touched by this review because she gave The Heartbreakers one of their first reviews.

Track Records

WALTER LURE: So we were stuck in England, and we had to do this showcase. It was after the Anarchy tour. We didn't have money, because the Anarchy tour was over. We had realized by then that the English scene is ten times better, 'cause people are getting serious record deals there and they're getting promotion. We figured we needed to stay for the one showcase gig because the buzz from the tour was enough to get all the record labels interested. The Clash and The Damned and The Pistols were already signed, so we had to get this one gig. And so, of course, it was the holidays, so we had to wait for the holidays to be over. We had to stick it out in London with no place to stay and no money for two weeks. The Clash put us up at their roadie's father's house, and we managed to scrounge around. We had this showcase gig, so there was all these record labels that came down; Leee was doing negotiations to get all the labels to come down. We did the gig, and then Jerry and me and Billy went back to the States and Johnny stayed. Within two weeks, we heard about the ones that were bidding, but Track offered us the best deal.

NINA ANTONIA: They start to get label interest, and who should come along but the same crew that was trying to sign the New York Dolls on that terrible night when Billy Murcia died—the people from Track. Now, what Leee and the band didn't know was that Track, at that point, were at war with The Who, and there was some money owed for royalties. So The Heartbreakers signed to Track, but they sign as The Chris Stamp Band. But anyway, it all seems peachy. At least they're going to be on this great British label that has all this history attached to it.

GAIL HIGGINS: Track Records was run by Kit Lambert and Chris Stamp—you know, two more crazy people! Wild people. And Danny Secunda and they were picking up this wild band so, you know…. As far as The Heartbreakers were concerned, how could it be better, as far as a record company goes?

LEEE BLACK CHILDERS: Look at the two owners of Track Records: Kit Lambert and Chris Stamp, Terence Stamp's brother. They started out with The Who, and Kit Lambert was a genius, but a complete junkie, and crazy and self-destructive. By the time we were working with him, he would come wandering into the office and you couldn't even make contact with him. He had no idea what was going on. He was so drugged to the teeth, and that's just the way it was at that office. It wasn't just the drugs, it was the attitude; the drug attitude of, like, they had Speedy Keen producing—wow! Let's just put all this cocaine on the bill!

My job, which I didn't want, was to look at the bills. And I was saying, "Wait a minute, there can't be a thousand pounds of cocaine charged to the band on the recording bills." And they weren't even *recording*, and this is all so legendary. It *aaall* fell apart. It was one of the most disastrous albums of all time. We know that, and now that it's been re-mixed a million times, we know that possibly it was some of the greatest rock 'n' roll music ever composed by some of the greatest—including Jerry Nolan, who was crazier than them all—the greatest music that you could possibly hope for. But just mis-management, including me, that just wrecked it all.

PHYLLIS STEIN: Well, it was pretty nuts up at that office; the inmates were running the asylum. The times were crazy, everybody was crazy! So I just figured, okay, this goes with the package. They were all…stoned.

NINA ANTONIA: The first single is "Chinese Rocks," which is a very blatant declaration of junkie life. They got some bad press. Charles Shaar Murray said that anyone that's singing about being on a Chinese rock deserves to be marooned on one. But if you listen to the lyrics, actually, would you want that life? Where everything's in the pawn shop? I would say that it was a warning. It doesn't stop it being a great rock 'n' roll song, but it's a warning nonetheless. You just have to listen to the lyrics.

WALTER LURE: It was Dee Dee's song to begin with. He had the chorus, the music, the first verse, and probably the second verse—"the plaster's falling off the wall…." There was a third verse that we used to do with Hell, but then we dropped it when Hell left the band because I couldn't remember the lyrics; neither could Johnny. Then Jerry told me that he had added the Buddy Holly drumbeat, the *bom budda budda dom budda dom,* which is possible, but you usually don't get a writing credit adding a drum beat to a song. Then he said Johnny added the middle break, that little sort of *bom bom bom* in the middle. Whether he did or not, I don't know, because it could be a Ramones thing. But again, you don't usually get a writing credit for putting a little piece of the song in, or something like that. But whatever it was, they wanted to be associated with a junkie song, so they loved it.

Dee Dee never gave us any grief over it because he couldn't get the song played with the Ramones anyway. The Ramones refused to do it. And it never really sold any copies, so it's not like there was any big money involved. He never bothered us or sued us or anything like that. I never read his books, so I don't know whether he said it was his song or not, but it really was, in a sense, his song—and especially as performed by us, 'cause we never used Hell's lyrics.

PETER PERRETT: After knowing Johnny for a few months, he started making suggestions about how he'd be much better in The Only Ones than John, and how about replacing John Perry with him. Although I was friends with Johnny, I wasn't gonna do something drastic like that. I think he appreciated my talent more than The Only Ones did.

BOB GRUEN: Johnny was a really good cook. I remember seeing him cooking spaghetti for the band in England one day. I have a picture of him in the kitchen, in his bathrobe, cooking up dinner one day. He was a good Italian cook and he liked to eat. Well, you know, *when* he ate….

He really did care for his kids. I remember one day he came over, I had some pictures of him and Julie. His son used to play with my son, and he used to leave his son with mine when we would go out together. I would have a babysitter or somebody watching them.

He could be a pretty normal guy sometimes.

WALTER LURE: In England, when we shared the house, Julie came over and brought Johnny, Jr., which wasn't John's kid to begin with. And Vito, and then they had Dino, or would come to have him. Julie would take care of them most of the time, but then there'd be these…big fights, you know? Johnny used to be running out buying drugs….

And then a couple of times the cops would come over, and John's in the bed, holding the baby, crying. And Julie's screaming, "He's a junkie! Look at his arms!" Blah blah blah. And the cops don't want any part of it. This is over in London, and we all shared the same flat together. The cops don't want to get involved in these family things at all. They won't drag him off into jail because he's got track marks on his arms. It would usually get resolved somehow or other, but it was a fucked-up relationship.

Julie was a piece of work, too. To me she was like, psychotic; she would change personalities from one minute to the next. But Johnny wasn't an easy person to live with either, so, you know, maybe they deserved each other. The kids, I sort of feel sorry for them. But we were too oblivious. They would come on tour with us.

PETER PERRETT: You didn't see him in control of the situation. They were kids that she sort of presented them to him. I don't know if he was even sure how he got them, you know what I mean? Like, he was with her and these kids happened, and he was just trying the best he could, musically. I mean, it's a big responsibility having kids. I'm glad I didn't have any at too young an age, you know? 'Cause, like, it changes your life.

L.A.M.F.

BILLY RATH: Back in the '50s in New York and Brooklyn and Queens, the gangs would write "L.A.M.F." on the wall of the other gang's territory. (There were different gangs, and that's [also] where D.T.K.—Down to Kill—comes from.) I kind of see it as Love And Marriage Forever. That's what The Heartbreakers were. "Like a Mother Fucker" was put on the gang walls. That's where it came out of. Jerry was very much into that, that gang type; he grew up in that atmosphere.

ANDY SHERNOFF: I love The Heartbreakers. They got one record, but it's a fuckin' great record—every song's a killer rock 'n' roll song. Every song was three chords. That's what rock 'n' roll's about.

BILLY RATH: *L.A.M.F.*, the recording: We went in, and they wanted it rough. We laid it down pretty quick. We didn't spend a lot of money at the beginning for the original recording. Speedy Keen was great. I can't forget the engineer…great engineer! We were pretty straight when we went in and did those recordings. Sometimes Johnny and Jerry might be a little late because they needed their medicine, you know, but they didn't overdo it.

PHYLLIS STEIN: We were in the studio—at least, I was with them maybe 3 or 4 times in the studio—and everything sounded really great. They were just knocking it out like a great live show, and this guy Speedy Keen, he was there, and Leee was there, sometimes in tears. But they sounded really great. And then when Track sent me a copy back here in New York and I put it on the turntable, I said, What…what happened? This is not what I sat there for days and heard. How did it get to be this muddy mess? I was really shocked about that.

WALTER LURE: Took us like, almost a year or six months to record that album. And we knew the songs like the back of our hand, so we kept on recording them over and over in different studios. Then there were the drug problems. They'd have a session set up at six o'clock, and we'd show at midnight…or some of us would be there and some wouldn't, depending on whatever the situation was. They put us up in nice apartments and they paid the bills, they were pretty good to us. They had parties at the offices for us.

I don't really know what the other labels would have done or not have done for us. I heard later on that a lot of them were sort of, "Well, can you control Johnny and Jerry?" when they were speaking to Leee. The reputation was already there, so they didn't know what they were dealing with; so it was legitimate. You know, "Why do I wanna deal with a bunch of junkies if we don't know if they're going to be able to make the show?" That probably played a part in the negotiations.

BILLY RATH: When we were recording this stuff, we'd do the drum thing, and then we were laying down some vocals. Jerry would just be off in the corner with his eyes closed. "Okay, Jerry. We need ya." He'd jump, you know? And sit behind the drums, do his thing, and then, "Okay." Then he'd go back and just sit there with his eyes [closed]. Yeah.

NINA ANTONIA: Johnny and Jerry had this kind of production hex hanging over them. They'd seen it with the New York Dolls' debut album, then with *Too Much Too Soon*, so they wanted to wipe the slate clean with *L.A.M.F.* And they were a great band, they were singing these great songs, but what they're recording in the studio isn't what they're hearing back. I don't know why they didn't go to their mastering process (although it's not obligatory for bands to do so).

So again, there are arguments in the studio. I think perhaps they were scared of a self-fulfilling prophecy of getting the production wrong for the third time. I'm sure that Leee has told you that Jerry begged to go back in and do the final mixes. And then Track came along and said they had to have *L.A.M.F.* ready for the Christmas market, so they had this deadline…. But the really sad truth of it is that they'd actually recorded a

Walter Lure, Jerry Nolan, Johnny, Billy Rath

PHOTO: PHYLLIS STEIN

superlative album, but every time it went through to the mixing process at the end, there was a problem.

WALTER LURE: We mixed it a million times. Twenty different people, including Jerry and Johnny and different producers. To me, the mixes always sound great. You play it in the studio, it sounded fine; so the levels were right. It was only when it got transplanted onto vinyl, you had this muffled sound like the whole thing was like compressed or muffled. And to me, that's not the mix. That's something else.

The pressing process…. We went to Abbey Road, to repress it there with the experts. We just didn't know what the fuck…it was like a curse. Our goal was to get the sound like the Pistols got on their songs; I love that sound, of their singles and their album. We tried everything, it just didn't work. To this day, I'll never know exactly what caused it. They mixed it a hundred times, but it always would sound the same when you put it on vinyl. So it just, like, got lost in the shuffle somewhere.

GAIL HIGGINS: Jerry complained through the whole recording thing. I have to agree with him; it came out like shit, you know? Nothing like they were like live, very under-produced. The sound is terrible, and Jerry was right to complain. Jerry was a bit of a perfectionist, so he wasn't happy about a lot.

BARRY JONES: Jerry was never pleased with the Dolls' mixes, he always thought that he could have done better. But Jerry was kinda like that, you know? He was very confident. I'm not sure that he could have made anything *that* [much] better.

I think he was disappointed that the power and how knock-out The Heartbreakers performance was didn't come across on the record, and he was right there. It sounds kind of flat. I mean, things like "Can't Keep My Eyes On You," they're just amazingly powerful songs and they came off flat. And he was very disappointed and angry, and they argued and they argued. Jerry, he's a very proud man; and he would up and leave. "That's it! You think you can do it without me, do it without me!" You know?

GAIL HIGGINS: He said, "I'm leaving! I'm going home." Of course Johnny was like, "What am I gonna do without Jerry? I can't have the band without Jerry; I can't do this without him." You know? And everyone tried to con-

vince [Jerry], and there were some reuniting, back and forth, in and out…
but that was the beginning of the end.

LEEE BLACK CHILDERS: I've worked with probably the greatest drummers in rock 'n' roll—through David Bowie, through Led Zeppelin…you know how many bands I've worked with. I've worked with great drummers. A great drummer is the most important thing in the band, 'cause he keeps the music going and he keeps it focused. A drummer is the craziest individual you could ever possibly hope to meet in your whole life. Do everything you can to never go near a drummer, ever, because they're crazy. And Jerry Nolan was [too]—and he knew it! Aynsley Dunbar knows it, John Bonham knew it. They all knew they were crazy, but there's nothing you can do.

Jerry was crazy, and plus he knew he was a genius; and he is, among all the drummers I've worked with, the most talented. Respect to his respect for the music. He knew exactly what to do to make a song work. He knew exactly how to carry it forward without taking over, without turning into one of those drum maniacs. He knew how to be the perfect drummer. He was my ideal in that respect. But at the same time, he was insane.

He wanted all the attention, and he thought because he knew how to make the drums work and how to make the music work, he thought he knew how to produce. Drummers cannot produce, guitarists cannot produce. Vocalists cannot produce. *Producers* produce. I've got to say it, much as I loved Jerry because he was *sooo* talented, the downfall of the first 88 mixes of The Heartbreakers' first album was Jerry Nolan. 'Cause it was all mixed for the drums. And you had Johnny Thunders' great guitar. Johnny Thunders was not the greatest singer on earth, but you had to hear him. There were lyrics. There was Billy Rath, who was not the greatest bass player in the world, but bass is so important.

The minute you start doing all that, it turns into mud. Mud, and you can't hear anything. The best albums—and, of course, the most legendary recordings were the ones done like that, and everyone said, "Goodbye." Gene Vincent, Eddie Cochran…they just said "OK, it's over with," and they walked away. *That's* how you do it. Because the minute you start to analyze it, it turns into crap, and that's what Jerry Nolan did.

PHYLLIS STEIN: [Jerry] quit the band because he hated the way the sound was on the LP, and I didn't blame him. I couldn't understand how this happened, and someone should have gone in there and properly mixed it—whoever's job that is. It wasn't really his, or any member of the band; because they like to put their hands on the knobs, and, you know, they go nuts. They don't know what they're doing; they're supposed to play the instruments. Somebody else should be doing that.

WALTER LURE: Jerry was never happy; he always had a negative beast in him. He'd be happy for a while, and then when it came down to the put up or shut up, he would say, "No, no, I, I don't like it. We got to do it again." So we gave [it to him]. Sure, that summer before it was released. And he worked a month or so on it. I don't think I ever heard it. Johnny or Leee was telling me that it was all drums and nothing else; what the fuck? But I can't believe Jerry would have just done that. In any case, no one liked it and so it didn't get released.

When it came time, it was October, and Track had called us in and said, "Listen, this has gotta be released now, because it's got to get out for the Christmas rush. Otherwise, you're gonna lose all momentum—and you're going to lose your contract." So we just said, "Fuck, you gotta release it." And Jerry said *no*; he was adamant. He said he'd quit the band—so he quit. Then we had to re-hire him and pay him a salary to come and finish the tour! We started the tour with a couple of others (Terry Chimes), but Jerry eventually came back and we were just like the same old band again, but he was making a salary. He probably made out better than the rest of us, but he said he couldn't live with it, and left. I didn't like it all that much either, but at least we still had a record company supporting us for a while, and hopefully we could have redeemed ourselves.

It's one of those things you look back on and you never get an answer for.

TERRY CHIMES: I'd heard about Johnny before I saw him. The guys from The Clash told me, "Oh, they're really good, this band. You should see them." After I'd left The Clash, they called me up and said, "Listen, we need a drummer. Do you want to come down and see what you think?" I went down to see them and I was very impressed with the whole set-up, the whole band. They sounded great, they really rocked. And I thought, "God, this is good," So I talked to them. Went to have audition, and we ended up playing together back in '77.

BP FALLON: What did the English audience think of Johnny Thunders and The Heartbreakers? They loved it. They really loved it. This was a real good rock 'n' roll band with good, good tunes. All right, so some of the subject matter was stupid and idiotic and showed their own Achilles heel, like "Too Much Junkie Business," but they made a great album in *L.A.M.F.* Of course the sound was dodgy, and so what? The sound is dodgy on *Raw Power.* The sound is dodgy if you stand in Trafalgar Square.

WALTER LURE: There was this whole sort of backstage scenario that we didn't know about that time. We heard later on that Stamp and Lambert were fighting over the royalties from *Tommy,* and they needed to prove that they were a functioning record company. They had us and they also had Shakin' Stevens and a few other people, but nothing major. And so that was their reason for going along, I mean, I'd imagine they would still want to be a business because the guys weren't retiring, but that was one of the main reasons they signed us, probably, to just to keep the label going—or hoping to get some buzz out of it. But that seemed to be one of the main reasons behind it.

NINA ANTONIA: Track Records goes bust, as we know. I think they just locked up the door. They stopped responding to Leee's calls. Leee has probably told you that he broke into the offices and got all The Heartbreakers tapes, which is a very Leee kind of thing to do. Completely left field, but genius nonetheless.

LEEE BLACK CHILDERS: Things were going crazier and crazier. What can I tell you? The reason we all loved each other is 'cause we were all crazy, but at the same time, you can't just *only* be crazy. So, sure enough, Track Records went so crazy that they went bankrupt. Me and Gail showed up ('cause we had a nice office on Carnaby Street) and there were big chains across the door and a thing saying we couldn't go in. The company was bankrupt; you couldn't go in.

Gail and I were standing there looking at the door and we knew that inside are all The Heartbreakers tapes. *All* of the tapes. Now Track Records did not own them. I had a really good financial manager named Peter Gerber. He had negotiated the contract so that no matter what happened, I owned the tapes. But the tapes were beyond all these chains and things. So we run out into Carnaby Street.

Now, Carnaby Street was then as it is now, a big tourist attraction; so there are tourists. We called my friend Mrs. Simpson, who was living with us. She had a 14-year-old son named Rocky, who was like a little gymnast. We called her and we said, "Can you come down here?" So they came down, and I looked at the front of the building and I said, "Rocky, can you scale this building and get in?" And he said, "No problem." So 14-year-old Rocky scaled the building, broke in the windows, got in. The safe was easy, 'cause I knew how to get into the safe. He got into the safe, came back and said, "What do you want?" And I said, "All The Heartbreakers tapes." In those days it was 16-tracks, right? He said, "There are 16-tracks of The Who, Marc Bolan, Jimi Hendrix, James Brown…do you want them all?" And so I called my business manager and he said, "Take only what belongs to you." Rocky threw 'em down to us. Right there in front of all the tourists. And we got all The Heartbreakers tapes. But right there was every single Who album, every Marc Bolan album, everything was all sitting up there…but we didn't take them. We took The Heartbreakers tapes. Kept 'em hidden under Linda Clark's bed for three years.

WALTER LURE: After the first tour and we found out that the record wasn't selling well, Johnny started getting managers talking into his ear. "Oh, go solo, you can make more money. You know, you'll do better on your own. You don't need these guys…." Blah blah blah. Whenever he'd play with us, we had to split all the money. People were whispering in his ear and he got the *So Alone* contract, the first single was "Dead or Alive." He stole the riff from "One Track Mind."

So Alone

BP FALLON: He was living in London, in D'Arblay Street in Soho above a so-called "massage parlor." And inevitably in the end he, with Julie and the kids, did a runner. And I don't know what possessed me, because it was run by very heavy people, but I went back there the following day to retrieve things; [from] teddy bears to Sid Vicious' bloodied bass. It was sad. Children's toys and the means of redemption melded in with destruction.

NINA ANTONIA: Johnny is approached to make a solo album. He's living in D'Arblay Street in Soho over a massage parlor—or underneath a massage parlor—and the office of Real Records is like, in the other corner on Old Compton Street. Real is presided over by Dave Hill, who was the Pretenders' manager as well. And Johnny was a real hero to him, and this is where the idea of the solo record comes about. You also have the Living Dead gigs with Sidney. He starts this kind of loose revue called The Living Dead, so you have a couple of The Only Ones, you have Peter Perrett, you have Henri-Paul. You've got Patti Palladin. You've got a couple of Eddie and the Hot Rods in there, and now and again you get Sid Vicious—I think, one time.

PETER PERRETT: Towards the end of 1977, Johnny mentioned that he that The Heartbreakers were splitting up, and could I help him get a new band together. I was great friends with him, and it sounded like fun and I wasn't doing anything. The Only Ones were between tours, I had time on my hands, so I said yes, I'd help him get a band together.

I thought of the name The Living Dead, which he was happy with, just as a working name. The Speakeasy had been an old musician's hole from the '60s and early '70s. And as we'd met in The Speakeasy, we started playing there. When Johnny started going there, it started being a cross-over, a meeting place between the new musicians and the old musicians. I think that's where Johnny probably met Steve Marriott and Phil Lynott. The Only Ones had stopped doing our residency at The Speakeasy, so we approached the owner, Jim Carter-Fea, about doing some Living Dead gigs there.

For the first gig, it was Johnny and me playing guitar. We needed a rhythm section, and the rhythm section I knew best was Kellie and Alan, The Only Ones' rhythm section. So we used them for the first gig, and Johnny really liked playing with Kellie, 'cause Johnny had a respect for what he considered *real musicians*. He knew Kellie's music from the '60s... even *I* didn't know Kellie's music, you know? I'd never heard any Spooky Tooth! I'd heard the name, but Johnny said to Kellie, "Oh, I love 'Dev-il Woman.'" Johnny was really happy playing with Kellie, and we did the first gig.

But after the first gig, Alan didn't want to do more gigs. Alan was somebody who was totally against drugs. He looked on Johnny as a being a fuckup, he didn't like his music.... Whereas I *liked* his music. You know, I didn't think he was as good as *me* at the time, but I liked his music. He was better than any of the other bands that I'd been to see around that time. The Heartbreakers were an exciting live band. So Alan didn't respect John-ny, and he told me he didn't want to do any more gigs after the first one.

So we were stuck for a bass player, and Johnny came up with the guy out of The Hot Rods, Paul Gray, and the French guy, Henri-Paul. And they were the two people who did most of the gigs.

There was one gig where Sid asked if he could play, and we had a re-hearsal. Johnny didn't want him to play, 'cause even Johnny had standards about musicianship, and Sid was below those standards. He just didn't know where he was. He couldn't even pedal an E, you know what I mean? He couldn't play [anything] all the way through. I had to get his fingers on the fretboard, trying to move them up and down. And Johnny said, "I'm not gonna let him play." It was obvious that Johnny was Sid's hero, you know Sid worshiped the ground he [walked on]. You know, it would have broken Sid's heart if he didn't play, after he'd been expecting to play. I convinced Johnny to let him come on for the first songs, and so we started the gig with Sid playing for the first three songs, but the speakers and amps were unplugged, so no actual sound came out. Sid had a great time for three songs—jumping up and down, being Johnny's bass player—until he realized there was absolutely no sound coming out. Even the non-musician he was, after three songs he realized there was no sound. So he started calling the roadies, and that's when Johnny called Henri-Paul to replace him. He was like a little lost child, Sid was. But he achieved an ambition by being on the same stage as Johnny.

JOHN PERRY: There was this kind of circle of people who would troop down to Island's studios at St. Peter's Square, where you might find yourself playing with people on Island Records or the few other people who were kind of part of this family; and I think that's probably the start of *So Alone*. Peter and John go down to St. Peter's Square, start playing. Ed Hollis, who was Eddie and the Hot Rods' manager, was there. Steve Lillywhite is there and that's probably where the plans for a solo album start.

PETER PERRETT: Dave Hill from Real Records…we'd had contact with him when he'd approached The Only Ones about signing us, when he was working at a different label. I can't remember who he approached first, but he knew me and Zena. He asked about Johnny and the possibility of making a record for Real Records. And part of the deal was that I was involved in some way.

Johnny didn't have a manager after The Heartbreakers, and he asked Zena to negotiate the contract with Real Records. Zena negotiated a contract that was reasonably financially rewarding. I can't remember exactly how much; it was close to ten grand. The Only Ones were getting around £40 grand at the time, but it was alright, it wasn't bad.

And then we got a sort of slurred phone call from Johnny phoning Zena up saying, "Sorry Zena, I fucked up." He'd gone and signed the contract and just got £700 in cash for it. Johnny had very sad eyes, and it made you sort of look after him and help him. I mean, all the times I played with Johnny, I never asked for any of the money that he was getting for the gigs, 'cause I didn't need it. I just wanted to help him.

NINA ANTONIA: So the core of *So Alone* is Steve Jones and Paul Cook, Phil Lynott, Steve Marriott, Chrissie Hynde, Henri-Paul, Patti Palladin, Paul

Nichol from Eddie and the Hot Rods, Peter Perrett and Mike Kellie from The Only Ones. It's this microcosm of people, the very best of the genre. But it's also a tribute to what Johnny means to the English scene as well. There's a lot of brilliant people on that album. The sound on that album is just absolutely wonderful. Steve Lillywhite....

Given the sort of failing circumstances, the tide was rising a bit. It's a great moment for Johnny, and there's a real purity to that album. It shows another aspect of Johnny, too. You've got "Memory" on there. You've got "She's So Untouchable." Yes, there were love songs in The Heartbreakers, but they're quite adolescent. [On *So Alone*], you're seeing a glimpse of Johnny the man, and you're also seeing a glimpse of the wounded hero—as well as the anti-hero.

PETER PERRETT: I felt that he felt the freedom to be sensitive. While he was still in The Heartbreakers, he felt he had to be the hard New Yorker. And I think that when he met me, he felt it was cool to be sensitive. I think I let him explore that side of himself, 'cause, you know, he was a very sensitive guy.

JOHN PERRY: Peter suggested to John that I come down and play bass, because they still hadn't got a bass player for the *So Alone* album at that point. I went down and put some bass on "Memory," but Kellie—if you remember the drum part—Kellie's playing this drum part off "Ticket To Ride," really. So I'm playing a sort of McCartney-esque bass line, but for John, it's "too many notes." John wants it dead simple. And part of his sound, you know, [was that] he had great bass players.

I think on *So Alone*, people who didn't get high would certainly have found John a problem to work with.

PETER PERRETT: When it came to do the sessions, I think we had two weeks booked. But we could only do the first week, 'cause The Only Ones had a tour booked. So I made sure that we got all the original songs done in the first week of recordings. That's "Can't Put Your Arms Round a Memory," "She's So Untouchable," "Ask Me No Questions," the title track "So Alone" and "Subway Train." We did all the original songs because, to me, that was what was uniquely Johnny. In The Living Dead we did some covers as well, but the covers were never as important to me, because anyone can do covers. Obviously they're done in a uniquely Johnny way, but it was much more important to do his songs which I thought were the best songs I'd heard of his, that bunch of songs.

And I enjoyed it. I found it a real freedom, not being the frontman in a band—having the freedom to knock about and have fun. Which you can do as a frontman, but there's a certain thing about singing backing vocals; it's a completely different thing. I really enjoyed singing backing vocals. I never considered myself a guitarist until Johnny said, "You play great, you're like Wilko Johnson playing machine-gun rhythm." I didn't consider myself a musician, even, and he made me feel like I was really contributing. And I'm really, really proud—you know, as proud as my own stuff—of what I did on *So Alone*. I think "Memory".... He might not have been the best songwriter or the best lyricist in the world, but "You Can't Put Your Arms Round a Memory" is a really heartfelt sentiment.

BILLY RATH: "London Boys." Well, the Pistols did a song that kind of put down the whole New York scene, saying that we were whimpers and didn't have it together. So me, Walter and Johnny sat down and said, "Here we go. We're going to let them have it now." They were all London boys, and that's really what they were.

PETER PERRETT: He'd done all the covers with Steve Jones and Paul Cook, I think, and they were finishing it off at Island in Basin Street. He wanted me to put some piano down on "Great Big Kiss," which I never actually did, 'cause I got really stoned to teach him a lesson. Normally *he* was the one who got really stoned and left me to do all the work, so just to teach him a lesson, I got really stoned.

He knew what he was doing to people, really. He'd get in a state and leave you to sort it out. And he knew he could rely on certain people to sort it out.

BP FALLON: Was it worth it? Yes it was. Johnny made the album *So Alone*, which he reckoned was his best record, and that was worth it. It's worth it for the music. You just keep on going. Was it easy? No. Was it horrible? No,

PORTRAIT BY JIMMY ANGELINA

because there was some sort of magic behind it all. It's not all negative, and it's still going, this music. From "Subway Train" to "Great Big Kiss" to "You Can't Put Your Arms Round a Memory."

PETER PERRETT: After the album was finished, to launch it, there was a Johnny Thunders all-star gig at the Lyceum. The strange thing, I thought, was that I was playing guitar, and we had James Honeyman-Scott—who was a fantastic guitarist—playing keyboards, you know? That's really weird, 'cause he was twenty times as good a guitarist as me. I felt a bit awkward playing guitar! I really respected James' guitar playing with the Pretenders, I thought he was a good guitarist. And there was talk of Steve Jones and Paul Cook turning up, [but] Johnny said to me that Malcolm wouldn't let them. I don't know if that's the truth. That's what Johnny told me, you know?

NINA ANTONIA: Now although The Heartbreakers had, by all intents, officially split up, they always were re-grouping. You have the great *Max's Kansas City* album which is, is in a sense with so much loss behind them.... I mean, I love the *Max's Kansas City* album, because the claws are absolutely out at that point. It's probably an ultimate punk rock album, because it's very down and dirty. It tells a tale, you know? That of chances lost once again.

WALTER LURE: Johnny wanted to get back together with us in New York; it was the *Max's* gig. It was strictly for cash. We'd do the shows and we'd make more money. We'd draw more people and make more money together than John would ever make on his own, even though he did decent on his own. The Heartbreakers drew more people.

So we would get together for these weekends at Max's, and we'd all walk with a nice chunk of cash for the weekend—enough to keep you in drugs for another week or two. So there was this sad [reality] that we loved. We kept on playing together, we loved the songs. But it was a cash cow for [us]. That's why I called my first Waldos album *Rent Party*, after the old Heartbreakers gigs. 'Cause you'd have a gig to raise the rent, or raise drug money, whatever you want to call it. It wasn't like we were writing new songs or anything like that; it wasn't a functioning band. We'd get together for these semi-reunions to play the shows, and we did these little tours—

up in Boston, out West a couple of times…. And then you start hearing the horror stories, you know, with John being in jail.

BILLY RATH: We did two nights in The Village Gate and we blew them away, because The Heartbreakers really picked up a lot of energy from playing with the punk rockers. We learned something from them and they learned something from us. It was a give and take. Because, you know, we played rock 'n' roll. The energy wasn't quite the same at the beginning as it was after we came back from England. The energy then was something else. People draw on your energy. They take from you but you have hundreds of people there throwing energy at you, you know? And that's why you see Johnny skip across the stage and do his thing. It was that energy that we created amongst ourselves, and we didn't like to stand back by Jerry's drums; because they're kind of loud.

Johnny at the very beginning, for the first big four years…a lot of it was show, as far as the drug. He would wait until afterwards. He would put that persona on, but Johnny had it together. Unfortunately, he started drifting. And the more and more he drifted, the farther he separated himself from us. And as I said, I had to get out of New York or I was…. The doctor told me, you have about two weeks to a month if you don't get out of here and get yourself together. I was gone in a week, and kept in touch with Johnny.

HOWIE PYRO: I was not old enough. We were all very, very young and for some reason Max's Kansas City and CBGB's at one point just decided to let us in, even though we were nowhere near old enough to get in there. So we started a band and I was in there. Early on, I went upstairs to the dressing room at Max's Kansas City, and I had this big mod watch I found in a thrift shop. It was like a bullseye. And I went upstairs and there were a lot of really hip people up there, and I didn't know a lot of them. I knew some of them, and I was, you know, ten years younger than all of these people.

Johnny Thunders was there, and I was all excited. And he was kind of being a dick. He was like, "Let me see that watch," and pulling my arm and wanting to see the watch. And then he was kind of like, "Hey, you should give me that watch." He was being all tough, and there was all these people around, and I was like, "Oh my god. What am I going to do?" And Johnny Thunders is like pulling and I'm just like, you know…! At one point I was just like, "What is this? This is retarded." I was like, "Fuck you. Get off." And he was like, *"What?"* He got all weirded out for a second, and he pushed me. And then everyone's like, "Whoa." And it sort of got like, "Oh god. Now I'm going to lose my whole world and be hated and kicked out of the thing I just realized I want to be for the rest of my life." But I pushed him back and then he pushed me back and I pushed him back, and then all of a sudden we were fighting and rolling around on the floor of Max's Kansas City and everyone's screaming and yelling. And at one point I realized that they are screaming and yelling for *me*, because he was being a dick, and it was funny. And I wound up…we were really fighting! I was this little kid, and Johnny Thunders is totally fighting. He shouldn't have bothered, you know. And it just was funny. I stuck up for myself and we got up and he really liked me, I think, because I did that. And he was totally like, "You're a good kid, you know." And that's how we met. And obviously I did the exact opposite of what I was afraid of; I kind of cemented myself in that world with all those people, and with him especially, because he really liked me.

Gang War

NINA ANTONIA: You have this sense of, "Ah, Johnny's gotten back to New York." But he does some shows with The Heartbreakers and he ends up in Detroit, where he runs into one of the heroes of his youth: Wayne Kramer, formerly of the MC5. Historically, one of the most explosive guitarists so…it's like Johnny's found a new *raison d'être*: He's gonna form a band with Wayne Kramer and they're gonna be Gang War.

BOB GRUEN: The Heartbreakers were on and off for years. I mean, they played their last-ever gig, and then they would play a reunion tour, and then they would play a farewell tour, and then they would get back together again…. But in between there was other variations, and Johnny played with Wayne Kramer.

Johnny went through a lot of different variations. He always managed to work. He always managed to have shows. He always had some very interesting shows. In spite of being pretty high all the time, he played very well. When he got on stage—which might be an hour or two or three late—he played a great show. He was always fun to see. So, he was always making money, 'cause he could always play these great shows. And that fed the habit. And he was always spending money, so he always had to keep working, and he never really got ahead of it.

CYNTHIA ROSS: Wayne and him…it was an interesting combination, because their musical styles were quite different. They both came from important bands. Wayne from the MC5, who Johnny really admired, and Johnny from the New York Dolls. And…it didn't really work out. When I think about Johnny, I don't really think about Gang War as his signature type of music. It wasn't his sound. And I think he was quite alienated living in Detroit, also.

WALTER LURE: The songs weren't all that great either, from what I heard. It didn't have any sort of spark to it. I mean, it should have worked. Wayne was a great guy, [Johnny] was a good guy, too. But it didn't have anything new about it.

MARCIA RESNICK: Johnny introduced me to Wayne Kramer, and I subsequently married him. He warned me not to marry Wayne and.... He announced the marriage on a record, but right after that announcement, he said, "You shouldn't have done it." He was right. As usual. Intuitive genius.

Johnny really respected Wayne's guitar playing, and it was really about that. It was about Wayne wanting to resurrect his career and Johnny wanting to do the same. It was about resurrection, I think. They were both trying to resurrect their careers, you know? That's what it was about, and it didn't succeed in doing so. However, it kept them making music, which was important.

You know, everybody has their lows and their highs, and this was a relative low, but it was a high for Wayne, because he hadn't been doing much at all, so.... It was a stepping stone. Gang War was a stepping stone for both of them, and it kept Johnny making music. Otherwise he wouldn't have, probably, at that time.

CYNTHIA ROSS: So when we played with The Clash, him and Wayne Kramer came from Detroit to the gig at the Palladium. They came to our dressing room, and Joe Strummer didn't want him there. There was Blondie and there was Wayne and Johnny, and Joe pulled me over and he said, "Cynthia. You have to ask him to leave." And I said, "Why? I can't; he's my friend. I can't do that. He came all the way from Detroit to see us." And he said, "I don't trust him." And I said, "He's trustworthy when he's with friends, you know...." And he said, "No, no, I don't want him in the dressing room." So I actually had to ask him to leave the dressing room, which was terrible.

He showed up later at our hotel, with Wayne. So we all shared one room. We had no money. Four girls sleeping in a double room on two single beds and you know, we pulled off the mattresses. Him and Wayne came to the door about one o'clock in the morning and they had nowhere to stay. So I said they could stay, but Wayne had to sleep in the bathtub and Johnny had to sleep on the floor. There was a limit to how much you could trust Johnny, and so I slept with my foot on him the whole night to make sure he didn't go through any of the girls' clothes or their purses or whatever.

I heard this rustling in the middle of the night, and I looked over and I said, "What are you doing?" He said he was rolling a joint. What he was doing was, he had the drawer to the night table open and he had taken the Bible out of the night table and he was rolling joints with pages from the Bible. And I said to him, "I thought you were like this good Catholic boy?" He said, "I am. I'm imbibing the word of the Lord."

PETER PERRETT: Another time we were both together in New York was the summer of 1980. He'd formed a new band, Gang War. I got together with him and he said, "I got a gig tonight, but I haven't got a band. Will you play?" And I said, "Of course I'll play!" He didn't explain the circumstances. Afterwards, I found out the rest of Gang War had a mutiny, [they] went on strike 'cause he wasn't paying them what they thought was their fair share of the money. Johnny obviously thought that he was the pulling attraction and that people were mainly coming to see him, and he deserved more of the money. Whereas he knew that I'd say yeah and I wouldn't ask for any money. So it was a much cheaper alternative, and he could stick two fingers up to them. And afterwards I found out that it was the last gig! They didn't even get back together.

In Cold Blood

BARRY JONES: After The Idols, I went back and worked at Max's Kansas City for Peter Crowley, doing the layout for the bands, booking the bands. Johnny was always hanging round the office, and I was there when he was about to lose his hand because he'd shot up something and it had gone bad. He had his mum on the phone in Peter's office, and he was telling her: "I can't help it, Mom, if I cut my hand in a cab door! Here, speak to Barry." And his mum berated me and made me take him 'round the hospital: "You get my Johnny 'round the hospital!" It was a good job I did, because they said if we'd left it, he would have lost his hand.

RICHARD LLOYD: Johnny and I did a couple of gigs together, mostly at the Peppermint Lounge, which was on 61st Street or something. Both of our guitars were in the same pawnshop on 8th Avenue and 46th Street. It was safer there than it would be with me. And I guess Johnny felt the same way. I always put mine in—even though the guitar's worth many thousands of dollars—I always put in for $75. So I went to the promoter, and would say before the soundcheck, listen, my guitar is in the pawnshop, I need 120 bucks to get it out. And he would fork it over and I would go get it.

Once, both Johnny and I went to the promoter at the same time and he says, "I'm not giving you any money. Show me the pawn tickets. That's all you're getting." We were like, "You're going to get a really crappy show out of both of us if you don't." We gotta get straight, you know? We would go get the dope, then I would go get the guitar, and then everything is cool.

BOB GRUEN: In spite of whatever drugs he was on, he knew how to take care of business. Of course he was pretty slick about it.

NINA ANTONIA: After Gang War, he's even deeper in the wilderness. He goes back to New York. I don't think these are good times for Johnny. He's surviving by his wits and it's probably a very tough life, but then he meets a guy called Christopher Giercke through Marcia Resnick.

MARCIA RESNICK: Johnny was staying at my loft. Christopher Giercke, who is a German director and drug dealer, was a good friend of mine. He had a loft near mine. He had a long table, and we'd invite many people over and have these gargantuan feasts, and I brought Johnny to one of them. Around the table, a mirror with white powder on it was being passed around, and Johnny scooped his spoon out of his pocket and brushed the powder into his spoon. Christopher had never seen anything like that before, it was new to him. Johnny ran to the bathroom and did what he had to.

Christopher came from a family of psychiatrists and he was very brilliant. He was very intrigued by Johnny, and wanted to know more about this fellow. Johnny was thrilled for all the wrong reasons about knowing Christopher, but they actually started to like each other in a very basic way. Christopher really adored Johnny's guitar playing and wanted to help him resurrect his career. He got him an apartment and gave him a salary.

Johnny was absolutely thrilled. He got a loft, right downstairs from Christopher. He had constructed a huge wooden cross for a performance, which he kept behind his bed. He was fascinated by crosses, obviously. He had a tattoo, and he was a Jesus aficionado on a certain level.

Both of them had a propensity for mischief. Christopher also liked dressing up. They had a lot in common, even though they were very different people. Christopher being from a Germanic intellectual background, and Johnny was more of a boy of the streets. They had a real fascination with each other.

Christopher knew that Johnny was not going to go anywhere unless he stopped using drugs, particularly heroin, so he did everything in his power to help him to stop, even if it meant using other drugs like methadone. He gave him the money to not be worried all the time, and enabled him to travel.

Nina Antonia: He brought about Johnny's renaissance as an artist, because if Christopher hadn't walked in then…then god knows what would have happened to Johnny.

Luigi Scorcia: Johnny had us booked at the Whisky, and we sold it out for three nights. The band flew down to LA. Johnny's still in San Francisco—bad fuckin' move. He comes into LA whacked out of his mind. We get on stage. I'm excited, the place is sold out. The first song. Boom. He falls down. I said, "You've gotta be fuckin' kiddin' me." I didn't know about that stuff, so I said to Johnny, "I'm going unplug your guitar." "Yay-eah, all right!" So I unplug the guitar, and we went through the motions and Tony C. sang all the songs.

Of course, the audience got fuckin' pissed. They started throwing things at me, and why throw things at me? I'm going to throw 'em back at them. Someone threw a Heineken bottle at me. Johnny said, "Don't you ever do that ever again, because they'll throw it right back on us, and we can't see them." That was one of the first lessons. See, Johnny was actually my teacher, you know.

We proceed to San Diego. Guess what happens in San Diego? We get arrested. We get arrested 'cause a young girl shows up in the dressing room who's in love with Johnny, sees somebody shooting up, calls the cops. And Johnny and I ended up in jail in San Diego for three days. Made the second page of the *New York Post*. My father says, "What the fuck is going on?" The funny thing about it was, no one bailed Johnny out. They bailed me out first, and when we were in jail, we were in separate holding cells across from one another and they had Johnny on TV: Heartbreaker Gets Busted, blah blah blah.

Simon Ritt: He was in really rough shape. He didn't have a record company, but at the time The Daughters were playing with him, he had some of the best material that he'd written in a long time. Songs like "In Cold Blood," "Sad Vacation," "Diary of A Lover." You know, he had great material; he always had new songs.

So Jim Nestor, our manager, was familiar with the Boston market and some of the studios in the Boston area, and was probably able to get a deal, get some recording time on the cuff. And that's how Johnny came to record in Revere Euphoria studios in downtown Boston, at Downtown Recorders.

Christopher Giercke, Johnny

FROM *MONA ET MOI*

Significantly, Johnny was going to work with Jimmy Miller. On paper, this should have been perfect. You know, the guy who produced the Rolling Stones? This should be easy. You know, Johnny Thunders — piece of cake, right? No way. When they were in the studio at Euphoria doing the basics, the engineer almost had a nervous breakdown. Johnny was bouncing off the walls like a pinball. He never did anything twice. He'd play guitar and everybody would rush out and get a guitar sound and then he'd decide he didn't want to play guitar, he was going to sing some vocal tracks. So they'd run out and change the settings, and then he'd go "I gotta go to the bathroom." 20 minutes later, he's back from the bathroom and it's like, now he's going to lay down some acoustic guitar, some bass guitar.

One thing that was interesting was watching him do the basic tracks. The basic tracks for a lot of those songs were just Billy Rogers on drums and him on bass guitar, before he overdubbed an electric guitar and vocals. A lot of people probably don't know this, but Johnny Thunders was a great bass guitar player. I think bass guitar might have been his first instrument as a kid and he played it really aggressively, a lot of body language. The way he played electric guitar was a thrill to see.

Getting back to Jimmy Miller, though: Headphones were being blown up. It should have been a masterpiece—Jimmy Miller and Johnny Thunders. Instead, Johnny's attitude was more like a kid being kept after class… 'I guess I gotta do this… I know I haven't recorded in a long time. To us this was a fantastic opportunity. We couldn't even believe that we were allowed to be in the studio. We supplied drums and amps and then we were half expecting somebody to say, alright kids thanks a lot, you gotta leave now but they didn't'… we were there from start to finish and even after Johnny left. Jimmy Miller salvaged a lot of stuff. He pulled odds and ends – you could see his experience… why he's Jimmy Miller; a man who makes a steak out of hamburgers. It was something to see.

CYNTHIA ROSS: The whole Christopher Giercke thing was a very odd partnership. Johnny was dependent on Christopher for a number of things, mainly money. And Christopher was dependent on Johnny. He was almost like a bloodsucker in some ways, you know? I didn't get a good feeling about him. I told Johnny that all the time.

He gave Johnny a place to stay on Laight Street. He had the loft, which is about the first time that he had his own place in years. And I just remember that there was no furniture in there. There was a mattress and a pile of clothes in the corner, and Johnny and his guitars. He used to call me in the middle of the night sometimes to come over 'cause he was lonely. He just wanted to play music, and it was a rough time. He wasn't sleeping. He was doing a lot of drugs. A lot of cocaine. I really hated the impact that had on him, 'cause he wasn't himself. He would become very paranoid about everything, and maybe with good reason. He seemed to be very lost during that time, although he wrote some amazing songs.

Hurt Me

LUIGI SCORCIA: We get to Sweden and it's a big thing and it's a huge place, sold out. Half of Europe is watching it live on TV, and Depeche Mode opens up for us. All right. We're about to go on, and I see Johnny's fucked up. He starts to play and he starts to fall down. He goes into the audience and he falls down on someone's lap.

After we do the gig, we get back on the plane, and Johnny's looking for drugs. So we rummaged through the first aid [kit], 'cause we heard that the Swedish people have heroin in the first aid [kits]. When we get off the plane—fuck! The Army or their National Guard had us surrounded. The dogs were sniffing us…we made the newspapers for seven days in a row, and the tour was canceled. Nobody wanted to book us, because our next gig was in Copenhagen. So we're stuck. Johnny's pissed. I remember him kicking out the windshield of a van because they couldn't get no drugs out there for him and Jerry's…. You know, they're both getting sick, because they need their medication. I felt real bad.

NINA ANTONIA: Christopher was making plans for Johnny's renaissance in each country in Europe, and he did that very well. Johnny looked like a little prince again. He had some great suits, he had his confidence…he was looking really good. So it all seemed to be on an upswing, really.

Hurt Me is a lovely album, because it shows that Johnny could be a serious interior artist. It's still a rock 'n' roll album, but again, it's more heart-on-the-sleeve, and it was commercially viable. The project with Jimmy Miller—the *In Cold Blood* album—and *Max's Kansas City* are not really comprised of songs you can play on the radio. But you could play *Hurt Me* on the radio. He could perform anywhere.

PETER PERRETT: Johnny got to a point where he'd do acoustic gigs. I thought [because] he got more money that way, rather than the artistic reason that he wanted to be a folk singer. He dragged me to a gig in Wardour Street—at Gossips, right? He said: "Oh come on then, let's go out." So I went out with him. He didn't tell me he was playing a gig. We arrived at this club, and he gave me an acoustic guitar that didn't have a strap on it. He said, "Come on, you're coming onstage with me." He just wanted me to mime, basically. It's hard to play a guitar that hasn't got a strap; you gotta hold it up. And you couldn't hear any sound; it didn't have a mic or anything. That's the sort of thing that you found yourself doing to help him out, but it was enjoyable.

TIMO KALTIO: He did a tour with Hanoi Rocks, and I was working as a guitar tech on that tour. I got along with Johnny really good. We sat together a lot [during] sound checks. He introduced me to his favorite drink back then: two parts of cognac and one part of Baileys, and you have to mix it just the right way so it doesn't curdle. After the tour, when he started doing other stuff, he asked me to come and join. And obviously, I did.

SAMI YAFFA: It was a co-headlining tour. I think it was in '83. We would play last one night, and then Thunders' band would play last the second night, and so forth. It was about two weeks and it was a friggin' blast. We ended up doing "Gloria" and "Pills" as an encore with either us on Thunders' stage or Thunders on our stage. It was a really good, funny, fun tour, man. It wasn't plagued by drugs, and everybody was top of their game, playing really, really well. We wanted to up each other, and that always helps. Nobody wanted to get too wasted and not be able to play.

WALTER LURE: I was involved with The Heroes and The Hurricanes… different bands. But it wasn't like a regular thing with John. John would be out of town and then he'd show up at shows and stuff like that, and we'd get together do a show. It was sort of rare. I had started working by '84, and I got a call from his manager, Christopher. They were doing this tour over in Europe, and they were going to film it at the Lyceum.

I got a week off from work, and we start with a show in Paris, and then a few shows outside of London, and then the Lyceum gig. The manager was doling out drugs to everybody. He'd give you your dose for the day, another dose at night. It was constructed chaos. And as soon as they do it, they'd be running around looking for more. It was just a drug-fueled tour, but there was money behind it. We had decent shows. The Lyceum show was great. I think I was sick as a dog when I did it, but it was a great show. And the tape was funny, too, what came out of it.

NINA ANTONIA: There was a Lyceum show, and Johnny appeared with Susanne, who he'd met when he'd done a Swedish TV show. She was a hairdresser. If you look at pictures of Johnny at that time, you'll see that his teeth go from being quite sort of junkie teeth to suddenly he has much better teeth, because of the Swedish sort of NHS [National Health Service].

So he'd met this Swedish girl, and in Johnny's head, Sweden becomes this clean, untouched place. It's Camelot. Avalon. A place that he can run away to, where there won't be any of the usual trouble. Anywhere where Johnny stayed for too long—NY, Paris, London—for one, two, three days maybe after he'd arrived, it would be okay. But then the drug people would start descending on him, and chaos would reign again. So Sweden seemed like this safe harbor, I think and that's what Susanne represented: A place where maybe he could live quietly. Breathe again. A place where there wouldn't be any problems.

BILLY RATH: I was living in Cape Cod. I was back in Massachusetts, getting myself together. Getting off methadone, getting off the pills and getting my health together. I actually went back to school. The state sent me back to Berklee, and I took up producing at Berklee College of Music. And Johnny got a hold of me there and said, "Do you want to go to Europe?" I said, "Okay." And I left the school and left everything.

NINA ANTONIA: The first attempt at remixing *L.A.M.F.*, all I remember about it was that the three nights seemed to be just one night. I remember falling asleep in the studio, as did Susanne, and Johnny sitting there at the

PHOTO: KATHY FINDLAY

control desk, saying, "Louder. Louder. Make it louder!" It was funny, but those times were good for Johnny. He had a lot of hope.

WALTER LURE: I was surprised, because that actually sounded good. The levels of the mix all sounded pretty much the same to me, except where Johnny decided to overdub and put [on] his own guitar solos, or Jerry's vocal on "Can't Keep My Eyes on You" instead of mine on there. But it was ten times better than the original, the vinyl *L.A.M.F.* And it might have been because of CD [technology].

NINA ANTONIA: So much happened in that period, it did seem for a short while that anything was possible. Christopher did try to sort of stabilize Johnny's chemical diet; there was a methadone script. I think Johnny was always at war with himself. I know that I'm telling the historical side, but I think Johnny was always at war with himself emotionally, and that before he could have come off drugs, he needed to come to terms with certain things. And he never was able to, sadly.

FRANK INFANTE: Christopher was working it, and working it good, you know? It wasn't just about getting him the money to go cop. It was more about like he had a *career* going, and he did a couple of films.

NINA ANTONIA: I think Christopher had put the ground work in on *Mona et moi*. That was with a French director called Patrick Grandperret, a very nice man. And the film won some sort of French prize and was premiered and everything. And Johnny enjoyed acting, as it were, although he was very much playing himself. But he enjoyed the experience of it, and it was widening the parameters of what he could do.

Que Sera Sera

JOHN PERRY: "Endless Party," "Little Bit of Whore," they're all recorded in Acton. Very professional sessions. There's stuff going down quick, and John playing live in the studio. At the *Que Sera Sera* sessions, it was still a two-guitar thing. He was a great guitarist to play with, doesn't over-play. Nice sense of time. The thing about John's style is that's it's the opposite of the image, which is flamboyant—he's big, bad Johnny Thunders from the Dolls. His style of playing is very tight. There are people who over-play, there are ungenerous players who tread all over your playing, and John wasn't like that. When he's playing lead and he's making his noises, okay, yeah, it's Thunders. But when you're laying down the rhythm parts for the things…. He was clearly someone who'd listened a lot to the Brian Jones-era Stones. That's always good to work with.

NINA ANTONIA: I do remember that there were pre-sessions to *Que Sera Sera*, and Johnny forgetting his lyric sheets and going to get them. He said, "Oh I've written this song about Billy Murcia." I was sitting in the cab with his notebook, bringing it back to the studio, and I could see all he'd written was two lines, and hadn't been able to take it any further. But his writing reminded me of Marc Bolan's writing. It was quite dyslexic. He was having a bit of a drama at home with Susanne and wanted to make it up. And also 'round that period, they release the "Crawfish" single with Patti Palladin. He basically spends 1986 traveling and touring, Japan, Australia, Europe, America…. First with The Black Cats, and then he splits with them and gets back with Jerry Nolan.

BARRY JONES: I'm in London, and I get a call from Jerry, who'd been in and out of The London Cowboys. The first year I'd played with Jerry was 1977. This would have been '86 when he called. Johnny and Jerry were both living in Sweden. [Jerry] said, "Do you want to go to Japan with us, in October? I told Johnny you're the best guitarist he could get." I'd been to Japan the year before with my band, The Cowboys, and it was a really great opportunity. I'm like, "Yeah." He said, "We're going to get you and Glen [Matlock]. We'll send you a ticket, do a week's rehearsal, and then we go."

NINA ANTONIA: There was a lot of excitement that Johnny and Jerry were playing together again. I interviewed Jerry at the time as well. Their relationship had been severed for a while, but they were back together. It was going to be 50/50, and it was going to be like it had always been. These sort of blood brothers were back together again.

BARRY JONES: The lineup with Arthur [Kane] only lasted for the American tour, which was two months, maybe. The biggest end was Europe, because we kept coming back and then going out again. It must have been a good month or two before the US came up. Glen hates flying, and Johnny and Jerry had a soft spot for Arthur.

Arthur was a real sweetheart. The last time I'd seen him was an Idols gig, '79, where we'd come from upstate or something in New York. We drove through the Bronx, and Arthur said, "I'll get out here. I'll see you later." And I never saw him again until '86! The band broke up, and that was it. But a very cool guy, you know? And then…well, I never thought about it like, *I'm playing with the New York Dolls.*

We did the West Coast first, and then we did Florida. The first gig for any of us in New York for a few years was this Ritz gig. And it was going to be big. It was Johnny and Jerry and Arthur back together. And I was on guitar, and I had a history there from The Idols. Anyway, we all had an agreement: We really wanted to show 'em that we're not losers, you know? "Johnny, *pleeease* don't get fucked up. *Please.*" Jerry was very adamant about it, and Johnny was in agreement, too. We were gonna knock 'em dead at The Ritz. This is the end of a year almost; we were a really good

PHOTO: XAVI MERCADÉ

band by then.

We had a couple of days off. I went back to his mum's with him for a day or so. It was really weird to see; just a classic Italian house, you know? We don't hear from him for a day and a half, and he comes back and he's been doing blow—coke. He's wired to fuck, and I think he'd done something else; he was slurring. Jerry was *pissed*—more than I'd ever seen him. Because for Jerry, it was really, really important. I was upset, too. Arthur was just Arthur.

We did the gig. Johnny kept blowing where we were in the songs, but we just kept going. We did the best we could do. I think that was the end of it for Jerry, but it wasn't finished until Johnny decided he was going to do an acoustic set, because he got more money than Jerry. That was it. It was a 50/50 split, and it'd always been that way, and it'd been that way for the year that I was touring with them. It was the condition that they got back together on. They bought me a suit in Thailand, 50/50 split.

Copy Cats

NINA ANTONIA: With each album, Johnny is showing a different side of him, but I do remember through the *Copy Cats* sessions a sense that things were not perhaps going that well in Sweden, and a feeling that Johnny was trying to salvage something. But he was terribly excited about being a dad. He was terribly excited about having a daughter, but I remember him telling me, "How am I going to cope when she has boyfriends? I'm going to have to follow him to make sure he's a good guy."

JOHN PERRY: *Copy Cats* stands out as a different kind of recording. I was in Spain, [and] this message eventually gets through to me sometime in late August or September: "You're needed in London." We fly back and they were recording at a studio in Camden. I didn't know the story 'til I arrived there; evidently it's a covers album. They're all songs I know. They're great, it's a good pick. They're gonna be fun to play. But they'd been in there two or three weeks with the first lineup of musicians, and it obviously hadn't been happening.

When I arrived, I came through this kind of courtyard, and there's John sitting on the stairs, head in hands, looking pretty despairing. The takes hadn't been happening, you know? These are songs that I know by heart. [So] Jungle [the label] got in a drummer from Gil Scott-Heron, and maybe the bass player—a rhythm section who play with good people. Patti's kind of overseeing the process, and doing a good job of it. It was fun. It was great.

NINA ANTONIA: *Copy Cats* was really well received by the English press, and it was good for people to see Johnny in a different way. He was also kind of experimenting with a different register in his voice, he was kind of singing a bit deeper as well. So I think that was a good PR move, almost.

John Perry: *Copy Cats* is probably the best sounding record I made with John; it had good engineers. There was a clear idea of what was wanted from the start. Patti was doing a great job of overseeing it and pulling in musicians from all over the place, I mean, the cast of different players on *Copy Cats* is probably as big as any record John made. Once she got the bit between her teeth, Patti was off, you know? They'd already gone doubly over budget for the record, and she wants horn sections. They get in horn sections. But then for some of the Puerto Rican songs, she wants castanets. So we have to have an Andalusian castanet player brought in. Poor old Alan [Hauser, Jungle Records] is tearing his hair out at this point, 'cause, you know, it's looking like [it's] going three, four times over budget. Patti ain't gonna back down on this at all. I think he ended up re-mortgaging the house to pay for *Copy Cats*. But it was a great sounding record, so it worked out.

Chris Musto: The first show on that tour was quite good. Second show, Johnny started losing his voice, and he got really nervous about playing London, which he often did. By the time we got to the Town & Country Club, Johnny was not in the best kind of condition, so we had to really beef him up. We got on stage and…he wore his pink suit, and fell over the monitors. And I always thought, *Well, if you're going to fall over monitors, do it in a pink suit.*

Sylvain Sylvain: Every year, some guy would come out and we would be offered stupid money [to reunite]. The only guy that never wanted to—because he was either too busy, or had contractual [conflicts]—was David Johansen. [The Dolls] were supposed to get together again back in 1989. We were all approached by this big promoter, and he was going to get us gigs. And when I told him David was not interested, he said, "Okay just you four guys"—Johnny, Jerry, Arthur, and myself. I tried to get everybody together, [but] the only guy that showed up was Jerry Nolan. And we started the Ugly Americans.

Johnny & Jerry

MARCIA RESNICK: I just think about one photo session I did with the two of them. It was so fluid, it was so lovely. Those two people really loved each other, and trying to visualize that love and put it into a picture was a joy.

PHYLLIS STEIN: The relationship between Johnny and Jerry was very special; a lot of people think "brothers." Sometimes, because of the age difference—Jerry being seven years older than we were—it was somewhat father and son. Johnny had a lotta respect for Jerry, because Jerry took no crap. And he'd be the first one to knock him on the side of his head and say, "Straighten up and get it together, or I'm not going out there." And that's how it was with Johnny. If you took crap from him, he had no respect for you. If you stood up to him and you told him, "You're acting like an ass," then he had respect for you.

BARRY JONES: Those two were fucking joined at the hip. Johnny needed Jerry's approval. Jerry needed to prove to Johnny that he didn't need him, but he *did* need him—so they were just in this locked battle for years. They loved each other, but I think they were jealous of each other at the same time, you know? Jerry thought he deserved equal billing to Johnny, and Johnny thought he deserved billing above everybody, including Elvis. But I know that Johnny really wanted Jerry to respect him as well.

WALTER LURE: Some people, like, Leee, used to say "unrequited love." To me, it was like father and son. Jerry might have been, like, five years older. Johnny was two years younger than me, and Jerry was like two years older

Jerry Nolan

FROM *MONA ET MOI*

than me, so there might have been about five years difference. But Jerry was the guy from the '50s; he could also beat the shit out of Johnny, which Johnny respected more than anything on earth. So Jerry more or less set the tone, and Johnny, he needed Jerry's approval. Later on, after Jerry got more attitudey, it wasn't as strong. But in the Dolls and even in The Heartbreakers, you know, Johnny would look to Jerry for approval for a lot of things. Like clothes, songs, style, stuff like that.

To me it was like a father and a son, 'cause Jerry was the only one who could tell him, you know, *shut up* or *fuck you* or something like that, and Johnny would do it. I remember once, Johnny was acting like an idiot. He was screaming or yelling at the waitress and Jerry just turned 'round and said, "You want a punch in the face?" And John goes, "No," and shuts up. It was like, an incredible sort of power. Jerry didn't use it that much; he let Johnny go and do whatever the hell he wanted. But every now and then, he'd get out of hand. I had heard that in the Dolls he used to take him apart and give him a little whack now and then but, but I never saw it actually happen in The Heartbreakers.

DONNA DESTRI: Tumultuous. I mean, they loved each other, I think. You know, like brothers. But just like any family—any band is like a family—there were fights. Jerry was a tough character, you know? Jerry was not a saint, nor was Johnny. But Johnny was good hearted. I think more so than Jerry. Jerry would take $20 from my wallet and I'd never see it again. Johnny would ask me to *borrow* $20, and he would come back and pay me back.

NEAL X: They went back a long time, didn't they? They were kind of old, old buddies. But I think there was a lot of anger there as well. But they were great. It was on fire. That was why it was great, you know?

JOHN PERRY: Jerry was really like an older brother. There were times when Johnny really looked up to Jerry. There were other times when he fucked him over on financial arrangements. I thought that was a shame, because they played so well together; Jerry could read Johnny's playing. But I guess you play that long with anyone, you kind of fall out, and John had periods where he needed cash badly so…. You know, shit happens.

NINA ANTONIA: In Johnny's last days, it was Jerry that he turned to. It was Jerry that he went to see. It was Jerry's counsel that he sought. So okay, they weren't working together again, but it was like people that had been married for 40 years. You know, even if they get a divorce, they still have to talk to one another. And that love is still there when it comes to the important things.

Oddballs

NINA ANTONIA: Johnny had always wanted a revue-style band. He'd been talking about that since 1978, when he first broached the subject of going to New Orleans and doing a '50s-style revue with a chick singer. He wanted to be a "grown-up" entertainer. He wasn't old, but he was getting older, and he probably wanted some easier people to work with.

CHRIS MUSTO: We went to Japan with Patti. Patti joined us on stage which was quite unusual. We did some *Copy Cats* material—"Alligator Wine" and "Treat Her Right." It was great having her around, she's hilarious. She was brilliant, you know? But then Johnny went back to America, and he phoned me up saying, "I've got these great guys, you know...."

In the meantime, we did a show in Düsseldorf with a friend of mine—a Scottish bass player—and a guitarist called Quin Patterson. And it's recorded, and it's really good. It was for a radio program. John was really on it, he was really hot. Anyway, Johnny went back to America and he phoned up saying, "I've got these girls and this sax player." I know he always wanted this kind of a big band, like the Duke Ellington Orchestra or something, if he had his way, you know? We were organizing stuff and I was meeting them at the airport. We just got on immediately, it was really easy.

ALISON GORDY: They had to put our name somewhere, and we had to think of something. And he just looked at us and he went, "You're such a bunch of oddballs." Then he just went, "That's the name." And we were like, "Oh, great."

CHRIS MUSTO: This [was] socially conscious, socially aware Johnny, who wanted to kick the kind of numbers like "Chinese Rocks." We got to a stage where we never played that song again. People wanted us to, sure they did. We did "Born To Lose".... But we stopped doing those, because Johnny was writing these quite sweet, twee tunes, you know, and listening to them just on acoustic guitar: "Okay, that's a cute song." And then we put them to the band.

Invariably, we hardly ever rehearsed with Johnny. We rehearsed as the band. And Johnny might turn up, but all our rehearsals were done at soundchecks and things like that. We decided to go for it, so we'd put a new song in like "Children," "Society".... He'd become this quite sensitive soul. Well, he always was. But in his songs...he'd suddenly brought this new light into them.

ALISON GORDY: He had written "In God's Name" with Patti Palladin. There was a book out, *In God's Name*, which he was reading, but I think Patti came up with more of the lyrics. "Children Are People Too," Stephen (my husband) told me there was a poster in the laundromat that was the exact words. "If children learn to be..." whatever, "...then they learn to hate themselves." You know, the whole lyric is basically the poster. "Society Makes Me Sad," he really did pen that. "Help The Homeless," I think Daniel Rey worked with him on that. But Johnny wanted to say these things, so he didn't really care where it came from. He wanted to perform them.

NEAL X: Last time I saw Johnny, I was in Paris, recording with Stiv Bators. We were recording at the EMI Studios, which is a real big studio. The Stones had recorded *Some Girls* there. We were in a big room. And it had been a really, really positive week, you know? We'd gone in to record three tracks, and ended up cutting most of an album. The band was on fire. They had a guy called Vom from Doctor and the Medics who was an amazing drummer and a guitar player called Kris Dollimore, who was really sensational. I was playing bass and some rhythm guitar, Stiv was singing.

Johnny came down to record some tracks that I guess they were originally going to play with Dee Dee Ramone. Dee Dee was going to be the bass player, Johnny the guitar player. Johnny and Dee Dee had a big, big falling out. Johnny came to the studios to do his bits, and it was pretty tragic. He was really wasted, you know? It was really sad. I remember he said, "Can you get me a really long lead? I just need to get away from myself." And he's kind of hiding in the corner. And then he played, and it sent shivers up and down the spine, because he just really had it still, you know? Even at his worst, kind of—stumbling, Valium-ed up—he still had something amazing.

NINA ANTONIA: It should have been a really good session, but there was an old beef that Dee Dee had with Johnny. I mean, he poured bleach on Johnny's clothes and he destroyed his guitar.... Johnny had so very little of any permanence at that point, he was living like a gypsy.

SAMI YAFFA: Stiv and Dee Dee and Johnny living together in the same pad and putting a band together? That's pretty heavy, man. Yeah, I think that they had some kind of misunderstanding and, you know, I don't know where it came from. But I know that Dee Dee, like, chopped all [Johnny's] clothes to pieces with scissors and then peed in his suitcase and destroyed his guitar and left. Something like that. I think there are many variations of it, you know, but that's what Johnny told me.

CHRIS MUSTO: A good little story on the guitar—the Junior—is, when we did the tribute album for Johnny (*I Only Wrote This Song For You*), the main icon was Johnny's guitar. I got his sister to send it over to us. When I got it, it was broken. Really, *really* broken. You know, the head stop was broken. The neck was off. All the metal work was off. And I had it restored. I went to Gibson, and Gibson knew it was an iconic guitar. They sent me to one of their top guys, and we had it remade—at Gibson's cost. We had it rebuilt and photographed. The last time I'd seen that guitar, Johnny was playing it.

BOB GRUEN: I remember when he said that he was really depressed that he couldn't see his children, you know, and that's why he was taking so many drugs. And I said, "No, you can't see your children because you were taking drugs before that. Your wife left because you were *on* drugs and beat her up to get her welfare money."

He had left Julie with two kids and she was pregnant with the third, and she was on welfare because he wasn't giving her any money. He came to get her welfare money and beat her up, and she called the police to save herself. And while the police were arresting him, she left town. And that's why he never saw his kids again after that. Not because she took the kids away, but because he drove them away. But I don't think he really understood that, 'cause he wanted to see his kids. He felt he loved his kids, and he felt that he was so depressed not seeing them; that that's why he was taking drugs. But the reason he wasn't seeing them was because he was taking drugs in the first place. So it's kind of a twisted circle.

I remember him telling me that. He said, "I need a girlfriend to care about me, and then I could clean up." And I said, "Johnny, look in the mirror. You look like a disgusting junkie. Nobody is going to go out with you like this. It doesn't happen that you get a girlfriend and then you clean up." I said, "First you've gotta clean up, and *then* you'll get the girlfriend." He wasn't ready to do that.

GAIL HIGGINS: He really wanted to have children, because those are people that will love unconditionally. And that's all John ever wanted, was to be loved. And especially, you know, when he had his little girl. You know, I remember his words: "This is a female that will never leave me." It really hurt him to not see his kids.

NINA ANTONIA: He'd split up with Susanne, so much went on in such a short space of time. I spoke to him before and after Hazelden. He was nervous, but it was something he'd had to do. But I think he also was doing it for his sister, you know? She was so thrilled when he went in.

There was a lot of people that tried to help Johnny. There was a lot of people that loved Johnny, but his drug use was something that he alone had to sort out.

But he took the plunge. He went into Hazelden. I remember it meant so much to his sister Mariann as well. But what she told me was that although he did the detox, he could not bring himself to talk about the emotional demons. He could not stand up in...I think they had NA groups going, and he just couldn't do it. He couldn't talk about the things that were pulling him apart inside.

Johnny always kept with him a picture of his sons. That was one of the first things he showed me. Anybody that came into his life, out would come this increasingly ragged picture of his boys.

GAIL HIGGINS: He was playing the Marquee—the new Marquee, in London—and he was in fantastic shape. He was like the old Johnny. He was, you know, so funny, so on form. It was like, *Oh my god, this is the Johnny I know and love from all those years ago!* And I went backstage and basically said that to him, and he said, "Well, I just went to rehab, so I'm clean at the moment." I said, "Oh my god, you're like the John I used to know." And he said, "Well, you know, I just substitute it with drink."

And that was the last time I saw him.

WALTER LURE: I'm not sure when he got the apartment. Not being around him all the time, I didn't really see all the trauma he went through. But he would stop [using] for a while, every now and then. It became less and less as years went on, but as soon as he got a minute—or he was bored or had nothing to do—he wanted to get high again.

Hazelden might have worked for a bit, but as soon as he gets back into the scene, it's a mental addiction. You have nothing else to do with your spare time than to just look to get high; it takes over your life like that. Where maybe when he was younger he would have sat down and wrote songs, or watched shows or hung out....We used to go and hang out at clubs, and we didn't have to be high in able to do it. But it became so consuming, that if you have nothing to do, you've gotta get high.

BOB GRUEN: The drugs take over your life, and it's very difficult to break out of that. I know that Johnny wanted to break out of that, but it's difficult, especially once you get a reputation for that, and people are trying to help you *stay* on drugs. People are showing up and giving you drugs.

I remember we were at the Cat Club. Johnny had just come back from Hazelden and he was clean for once in his life, and he wanted to stay that way. And some kid at the bar came up to him, said, "Hey Johnny, want to smoke a joint?" And Johnny said, "No, no, I'm not doing that anymore." And the guy looked at him and said, "What good are you then?" And walked away.

So Johnny was under that kind of pressure—that people didn't even want to talk to him if he wasn't on drugs. That's what people liked about him. That's what people heard about him. They came to see how high he was going to be, and eventually he played on it, you know? They had advertisements—"Catch Us While We Are Still Alive." Which was prophetic, and it ended up being true.

RACHEL AMODEO: I asked him if he would do the soundtrack for my film *What About Me*, and he said, "Yes, I would love to do that."

We were looking at the footage so he would get an idea of what music would go in what parts of the film, and then one day he came and said, "I'd like to be in your film." I said, "Oh you would? That would be great." 'Cause I didn't think to ask him. And I said, "Well, you've seen the film so far"—'cause I think I had probably almost an hour together. I was shooting it like a soap opera. I'd add things depending on when I had money or when we could get a camera for free. It was definitely guerrilla filmmaking at its most genuine.

He came over and told me that there were two things that he would like to be in the film, and that would be either a priest, or my brother. I said, "Well, maybe you should play my brother, 'cause we're both Italian. We both have dark hair. Not that we look alike, but we could probably pull something like that off." And he says, "Okay, that'd be good." And that's how I wrote him in there.

WALTER LURE: Jerry eventually got away from needles and all, but he was on methadone for like, the last 30 years of his life. Johnny never stopped. I mean, when we had our reunion show in 1990, six months before he died (it was November, he died in April '91).... We rehearsed a few times before it, just to see if we remembered our old songs. We had Tony [Coiro] on bass, but he was straight too, and the rest had all gotten away from it. But Johnny shows up late, goes to the bathroom, he plays two songs, he's got to run back to the bathroom again. It just never stopped, and Johnny never got out of it. Which is was always amazing that he lasted as long as he did.

He used to show at the Continental all the time, whenever the Waldos were playing. He'd be in the audience, and I'd say, "John, want to play a song?" Yes, he wanted to play the song. This is before the show. "Yeah, wait around, I'll call you up, you know?" And usually for guests, you wait 'til the end of the show, because you want to do your own stuff. But Johnny'd be out in the audience, making a big deal: "Yay, Walter, let me on stage!" So he'd come up on the second fucking song. And he'd play a few songs and then, you know, get the crowd all excited, and then he'd leave. So, it'd be like, he would do it deliberately, just to annoy. 'Cause then you have to pick up where you started, start all over again. And you're supposed to save the big sensation for the end or whatnot. So that's typical of John being annoying. But that used to be fun. He would do it all the time.

SAMI YAFFA: I talked with him about going on the road, but I think he had been on the road for a couple of months by then, so he was really tired. He said, "I hate going on the road." And I was like, "What do you mean?" "I hate it because people just come to see me getting fucked up." And then I was like, "Well why do you get fucked up?" And he was like, "I don't know," you know? But he was definitely aware of that factor, that people just came to see junkie Johnny play, fall over on stage, and have fights with the audience, you know?

CYNTHIA ROSS: We stayed in touch. I had gotten involved in the drug scene, as most people did in our scene in New York, and I had been clean for quite a while. A year after I got clean, he came to Toronto. I think he was living in Sweden by then, and he was with Susanne. He called me and he was doing a show, and he said that he just wanted to see me one more time, and make sure that I was OK. It was very eerie, actually. And I thought about that a lot in years to come; you know, after he died. Like, what did that mean?

SYLVAIN SYLVAIN: The last time I saw Johnny, he came to see me. It was on Houston Street. It was the same guy from the Continental Divide who opened that club up, and I was playing there and I had, like, an all-girl band. And he came in with Rachel [Amodeo], the movie-maker. But he was really saying goodbye to me. And he was really telling me like, you know, "I'm sorry it didn't go the way we wanted it" kind of a thing. He said, "Sylvain, man, you want to smoke a joint?" And he had this *huge* fucking [joint]…it was mainly tobacco, anyway. We sat in the little dressing room, it was like a closet. And he said to me, "You know, *maaan*. You taught me everything that I know…." And he really shared some beautiful words with me, and really touched me. I told him, "You know I love you, too." And we both hugged.

He was really humble about his life. He was trying to kind of put it all at peace. I really do think he knew he didn't have long to go.

MARTY THAU: Last time I saw Johnny, he was appearing at Irving Plaza, and I went backstage and I saw him. He gave me a big hug, and "How nice to see you, Johnny" and everything. And I'm looking at him and I'm seeing green spots on his face and I'm thinking, *Oh my god this is like, terrible. The way he looks.* He looks terrible, and people wanted to see if he was going to live on stage or die on stage. It was kind of sad. Pathetic. But supposedly…I don't know, supposedly he went to Japan….

SAMI YAFFA: I think, like a month before he died, we were doing some kind of thing with Michael Monroe at The Limelight, and [Johnny] was in town. He said he was going to Japan to do a tour, and he thanked Michael. He said, "Without Hanoi Rocks, I don't think I would be having this friggin' career in Japan that I'm having right now." We did really, really good business over there, and they realized who were our influences and all that, and got hold of Johnny. I think it was Smash Corporation who did it.

He just came to say hello. We had a couple of drinks, he had his White Russian, and we just sat there in the VIP area of The Limelight in New York and wished him bon voyage.

Showdown

PHYLLIS STEIN: Johnny was having a really hard time getting himself to Japan. Day after day, he wasn't getting it together to make the flight, so Jerry went to visit him. That day was the last day they saw each other. He came home and said to me he didn't like the way Johnny looked. He said Johnny seemed very frail and weak and he had bruises all over his body in places where he shouldn't have had them. When I was 19, my mother died from acute leukemia, and that's the major symptom; that, and fatigue.

I said to Jerry, "I don't like what you're telling me. I know that this is going to sound crazy, but this sounds like he's got acute leukemia." Jerry really didn't even understand what I was talking about. I said, "That's not a good thing." He said, "Another thing I didn't like about it: We shook hands goodbye in the exact same place on 14th and 3rd where we met—the day I joined the Dolls—and he was going to bring me up to the loft to pick clothes, do things like that."

It really bothered him that he said goodbye to Johnny the same place he said hello to him so many years earlier.

JILL WISOFF: When he left for Japan—and I was with him that night—when they came to pick him up, he was 85 pounds. He had sores all over his legs, which may or may not have been from leukemia, which they said at his autopsy he had. It's very possible. He was in tears, because he knew he had to go back and get help. He needed to go into a hospital.

I said to him, "John, you're going to have to not do this tour and go into a hospital." 'Cause he said, "Jill, Jill, can you help me? Can you help me?" I said, "I can't help you. It's your own decision." But he was so in fear that if he didn't do a tour and fulfill his obligations, he would never work again.

ALISON GORDY: He was quiet. Usually we would have a day and hang out or sightsee. [Tour manager] Mick Webster was getting doctors for him. I don't think it's easy to get drugs in Japan, I think it's pretty hard. Drinking is probably the best you can come up with, but he wasn't really doing that either. He was very quiet. The shows were good, but he was very subdued and he was very pale.

CHRIS MUSTO: In Japan, he came up to me one day and he said, "Feel this." You know, it's this lump on his neck. And I said, "Johnny, you're looking a funny color as well, man." He looked ill, you know? He'd looked pretty thin as well. And he said to me something like, "I'm not well. You don't really know how ill I am."

ALISON GORDY: The last time I talked to him was in Japan, in the lobby of our hotel. The boys were going to Thailand to do acoustic stuff. Last thing I said to him was, "Write to me from prison," because I figured they'd arrest him over there. Jamey told me he almost went to jail several times. I mean, it wasn't good.

And they finally got him on the plane and got him home, and as Jamey also reported: "This was the first time I'd ever really met the airplane's pilot," who came back to tell him, "If your friend doesn't quiet it down, we're going to land in the Aleutian Islands and drop him off. So get a grip." I think they got him a sleeping pill and knocked him out.

My husband saw him when he came back to New York after Bangkok, he was there for a few days. I picked up the phone, and Johnny was like, "Yo yo yo yo yo! *Let me talk to Steve let me talk to Steve let me talk to Steve!*" "Okay, here." Stephen went over to see him, and that was the last time he saw him. Then Johnny took off for Europe. Did the thing with Die Toten Hosen, then he went to New Orleans.

BOB GRUEN: I saw Johnny in the spring, I guess it was around March. He died in April, right? So I saw him before he went to Japan. We were hanging out together. He was pretty deeply into heroin and cocaine, shooting them both together. You get pretty whacked out, you know, kind of speeding and nodding at the same time. It really puts you in a very strange situation.

And he went to Japan, and I remember thinking like, maybe he'll be able to clean up. Because in Japan it's very hard to find drugs, but apparently the promoter found him enough substitute pills or whatever to get through with his habit so he could spend a week there. He made a lot of money, and then went to Bangkok where drugs are cheap and very available. He also bought a bunch of suits, and he bought a lot of drugs, and he came back to New York.

I was pretty clean at the time and he knew that; I'd even stopped drinking. He called me about 8:30 in the morning and asked if he could come over for breakfast. (He knew I was one of the few people he would know that was awake at 8:30 in the morning.) And I remember thinking, *Oh man, he's up early. Maybe he's cleaned up from this tour.* We went to meet over on Christopher Street, at this place that had a really nice brunch, breakfast place. And he came walking down the street. From about 8 feet away, I could smell the cocaine sweating off of him. And I realized that he'd been up all night or several days, and that he was really kind of whacked out.

We sat down and we're having breakfast. I remember he was talking about going to England. And then he wanted to get some Methadone, so that he could get off the drugs. And he was going to go to Germany, where somebody had hired him to produce a record. He was going to get some more money, and then his plan was to go to New Orleans and clean up down there, use the Methadone to get off the heroin. And he wanted to find musicians in New Orleans and do an acoustic album. He wanted to find old blues musicians—New Orleans has more musicians per square inch than any other place on earth—and that was his plan: To do a nice acoustic [recording] with New Orleans musicians. And it sounded like a pretty good plan, because he really was messed up. But I liked the fact that he knew it, and he knew he wanted to clean up.

It was also interesting that he remembered—even though I had forgotten—that a few weeks earlier he'd borrowed $50 from me. At that breakfast, he took the $50 out—he actually had a whole bunch of like, hundreds and fifties, kind of crumpled up, you know…. It reminded me of the way strippers get dollar bills and they just crumple them up and stuff them all into their pocketbook. Well, he had all his money stuffed in his pocket, but it was like hundreds and fifties. And so he would take one out, and two or three others would fall out. And that wasn't a good thing to do in New York City, and it certainly wasn't a good thing to do when he went down to New Orleans a week or so later.

New Orleans

STEVIE KLASSON: He'd just signed a new record deal in Japan, I can't remember with what label. But the plan was to go to New Orleans, hire Sea-Saint Studios—which is a legendary old studio in New Orleans—get Jerry Nolan back on the drum seat (and you know, some of the old boys were going to be in the proceedings), hire some musicians from New Orleans, and make a new record. That's why we were moving our base to New Orleans. But you know, Johnny went down there and died.

GAIL HIGGINS: Any drug death I think is going to have lots of speculations. Johnny, Elvis, Marilyn…any of them. No one's ever gonna know the truth, except for him and whoever this person was who was there. So do I think that something was fishy? Possibly. Do I think it was just the drug OD? Probably. Don't know the answer.

ALISON GORDY: Honestly, I think he really was kind of wanting to wrap it up with this lineup. Not because he hated us; just because he wanted to do something different, and Stevie [Klasson] was the most free person…. He was very young, and he was ready to go anywhere and do anything. Johnny had talked to me, said, "I wanna do songs from every decade—like 1910, '20, '30, '40, '50. I wanna do songs like that. I envision having, like, a big, black choir, like the Edwin Hawkins Singers." You know, that kind of thing.

PHYLLIS STEIN: Tony Coiro called me; the call came at night. Jerry had gone to sleep, and I got the call about Johnny. I woke him up. I said, "I have something to tell you." I didn't know how to say it. There's no good way to say such a thing. So I just said it. And he said, *"No!"* and he walked out of the room into the bathroom for five minutes. Came back in and said "What happened?" And I said, "Well, I don't know that much about what happened because *they* don't know." It was bad. [Jerry] went into a big depression.

PETER ORR: My brother tells me Johnny has been killed in New Orleans. And the way my brother told me, he was hanging out in this punk rock bar—Kagan's—and he met these kids who recognized him, and he invited them back to get high with him. My brother told me they hot-shotted him and took off with his shit. When I finally came here, I specifically went to Kagan's to look at it. These are just half-assed punk rock kids. If you claim to be a punk rock kid, why would you kill Johnny Thunders? Particularly *deliberately.* This is like, "I'm into the Stones, I'm going to kill Keith Richards." Why would you do this?

MARTY THAU: Supposedly he had $20,000 in his pocket, and next thing, he's dead. Mariann Bracken, his sister, brought up a good point: That the New Orleans police didn't bother to investigate his death, thinking, "Ah, what the hell. He's a rock 'n' roller. Junkie. You know, who gives a shit, he's dead. Let it be." But meanwhile, his passport, his guitars, his clothes—and the $20,000—they're all gone. And yet there's no investigation.

Supposedly, some real wise guys down the hall met up with him, saw that he had drugs with him, or methadone, and offed him. And that was the end of Johnny Thunders.

NINA ANTONIA: Having read the coroner's report and having researched as best as I can from talking to family members, Johnny didn't die of an overdose. You see it written down over and over and over again in the press that Johnny died from an overdose, but there weren't enough drugs in his body to constitute an overdose. There were traces of cocaine and methadone in his system. A coroner would report this, but the report also states that the amount found wasn't lethal.

He was ill. He had lymphatic leukemia, so all those terrible lumps and bumps that worried everybody…he was a very ill man. I suspect that he may have been hanging out with lowlifes, and that his room was systematically ransacked while he was dying.

I hate to think of him being alone. He was somebody that didn't like being alone. Not even for one night.

SYLVAIN SYLVAIN: I disagree with, you know, the people in New Orleans, or Johnny's sister, saying that all those guys killed Johnny, and all that. I disagree with all that. He was going. He was gonna go.

WALTER LURE: That was the obvious thing. He was heading for that. I was surprised how long it lasted. 15 years from the start of The Heartbreakers to when he finally died. He was in pretty bad shape by the end of The Heartbreakers. So he'd been living that way for 12, 15 years.

RACHEL AMODEO: Well, I'll tell you a funny little story which might seem freaky to people, but….

I'd heard about this famous medium that lives out in Huntington, Long Island. He has a couple of books out. I made an appointment for me and Mariann to go see this medium, because he apparently communicates with people that have moved on. My brother had passed away, and Johnny had passed away, so both of my brothers, in a sense, passed away in my life.

So Mariann and I went to see this medium. And the minute we sat down, he said, "There's a male on your right side, and there's a male on your left side. There's two people, and they're male entities." And I knew it was Johnny and my brother. I'm sure of it. But Johnny did say to me and Mariann—through this medium—that there was no foul play in his death, and that basically, the blood vessels, the blood cells in his arms, went a little crazier, like radical, and he died from that. He just drifted off. One minute he was here, and one minute he wasn't in his body anymore. He said that it was a peaceful passing. That it was no foul play, like all the conspiracy theories that were going on about his death. And I believe it.

Mariann was very skeptical, going with me; she didn't believe in any of that. [But] the medium was able to pick up on a couple of very personal issues that nobody else knew about, and she was in tears. She basically believed it. And I'm kind of a sucker for those things, too.

I Only Wrote
This Song for You

GAIL HIGGINS: We always used to say, "You're either *on* the bus, or you're *off* the bus." And Johnny was always *off* the bus. He really wasn't capable of being happy, and he really, really wanted to be. He didn't want to take drugs, and he was never strong enough to stop. He was 38 years old when he died. You know, that's so young.

His legacy is so strong. He was a fabulous performer, more charisma couldn't be had. So many people now give him credit for that.

LENNY KAYE: Johnny was the essence of rock 'n' roll. There was a purity to him. If you took the sound of the electricity coming out of the amplifier and through the guitar and bottled it, you'd have the spirit of Johnny. There were other players who were more technically accomplished, but hardly anybody ever looked as good as Johnny playing. And he had a sense of desire to him that really converted him into this pure rock 'n' roll embodiment. He had such flair when he played, such a sense of belief in himself and the music that could set him free.

JOHN PERRY: When he wasn't playing, I always remember him just hanging out, watching videos with us. People have an idea—because the Dolls hit early, and because of this kind of image of big, bad John—people think he's this tearing-'round-town guy. But he was a private guy. Jayne County describes him as being like a little kid, and that's true. There was a real sort of little-boy side, a vulnerable side, to John. But equally, I mean, he knew how to work that. When he needed something, he could exploit that—the big, brown eyes, and poor Johnny…. He could work that a dream.

WALTER LURE: He was unique. I mean, I knew him for years. John could get away with anything. He had this special personality. He could be charming and obnoxious at the same time.

Nobody else played like John. He made this weird noise that no one else could make. I tried it on stage. He'd start to sing, and I'd take his guitar because I'd break a string, and I'd play—and it wouldn't sound the same. It was a totally different sound. He was limited in his scope, but what he did, he did like no one else; so that's what made Johnny special, musicianship-wise.

Personality-wise, he was an outside personality. Probably because he was a little guy, he had what they call a Napoleonic complex. He was always talking louder than the rest, and he had to have his amplifiers louder than me. So there was this fight between us for the whole five years we played together, over who's going to get the loudest amp. And we'd pile amps on top of one another…we'd try all tricks, and we'd constantly razz each other about it, so it was sort of funny. We wanted to change his name to Johnny Volume from Johnny Thunders, because he was just like noise left and right.

He would do whatever he wanted, because he didn't give a shit. And he would usually get away with it, because people felt they wanted to take care of him; and that's probably why he got so screwed up in the end. People just let him get away with whatever he did, and he just never stopped. And whenever he started, he kept on doing more. So…he just went over the top.

JILL WISOFF: I could say, without a doubt, John's understanding of himself was as an entertainer. But his passion—and what he'd want to be remembered for—was his songwriting. He was very proud of his songwriting, and he worked hard at it. I say this also as a songwriter, that I learned a lot from him.

SAMI YAFFA: The guy was an amazing songwriter; you can't get over it. You know, his songs are classics, and will just go on and on and on. Even though they didn't sell that much, they are probably some of the most influential songs that there are. Look at the New York Dolls songs that he wrote, and The Heartbreakers, and his solo album. Those are records that will stay in rock 'n' roll history forever.

BARRY JONES: He was an innovator. It's like Chuck Berry was special in the guitar, the way he opened up rock 'n' roll. Johnny took it that step further.

PETER PERRETT: He had enough confidence to be himself the whole time, and he didn't fall for society's con that somehow drugs are evil and that there's a war against drugs.

BILLY RATH: I am glad that I was able to be part of it, because I want the world to know this other side of Johnny. He wasn't just a druggie; he was a *man*. He was a songwriter. He was a gifted musician, and people today can't write like he wrote. He was another Bob Dylan. You know he would come out with songs like *that*. I don't know how he did it.

And as far as his guitar playing…boy, no one could touch him. I mean, he'd hear the blues back from the '50s and the '40s…if you listen to blues, you'll hear Johnny in there. But Johnny didn't copy them, and they didn't copy Johnny. It's just Johnny had the blues. He was a bluesman. A rock 'n' roller. An incredible person.

PHYLLIS STEIN: I think what set Johnny apart from most of the other people that came out of the New York scene was the fact that he was so prolific. He was such a great singer/songwriter. Very few of the people in the bands he played with were able to write songs like that, and that's really what set him apart.

Other than his unique talent, he always had a great style. He always knew how to put clothes together. Jerry, too. They were both into it so much. It took them longer to get dressed sometimes than it would take me, and things would be pulled out of the closets and traded and tried on. It was part of life with them. It wasn't a put-on. Everything was for real, and it was fun.

NITE BOB: I'd say he had a big, outgoing personality. A harsh, primitive guitar style, right? And I also think that he struck a responsive chord with people, because that's why people are still thinking about him now. Something about his personality and his look. People either wanted to be like him, look like him, or sound like him. I guess it all came from the heart. He put his whole being into when he played and the way he looked.

TERRY CHIMES: Johnny was very talented, more talented than his record sales would show. He played the guitar brilliantly. I loved his style of guitar playing. He sang brilliantly. He sang with a lot of heart, and he wrote great songs; so he had all the ingredients, and he looked great as well. Not many people have all those ingredients in place. Johnny could have been a much bigger star than he was. With hindsight, Johnny could have been massive, but I don't think he wanted that.

MARCIA RESNICK: There was never a dull moment with Johnny. He was always getting into mischief, and encouraging everybody around him to do the same. He was so charming. And because he was so charming, he could get away with a lot. He was like a little boy. We were like brother and sister.

LENNY KAYE: People forget how tender he was in a certain way. As a solo artist, you got a sense of his vulnerability, and that to me is what made Johnny beautiful; the fact that he did give you his heart. He really did. He did open his heart through his music. He caused many problems for many people, but mostly he caused them for himself. And because of that, he was able to tap into an emotion that was real.

NINA ANTONIA: He had so much charisma. Wherever you were with him, he was just different from regular people. He just radiated this charisma, this cool and...*attitude*. But he did also have a heart, which was why he was ultimately lovable. Johnny was like somebody that was always in the best movie that you've ever seen.

BOB GRUEN: I always felt that he had a tremendous influence on all the guitar players that came after him. It's hard to hear any kind of rock 'n' roll band today that doesn't play some of those bending, high-pitched Johnny Thunders notes. And I remember telling Johnny one day that I thought he was like the Chuck Berry of his generation, and he ought to clean up, because he was such an inspiration to these kids. And he said he wanted to, but it was just, you know, really hard to do.

SYLVAIN SYLVAIN: I love Johnny. I wish we had time for me to tell you all the stories and all the great times. But heroin changed the course for him, and for me with him, and for the Dolls. I don't think David Johansen could have stood up and said, "Hey, you're all replaceable" if we were really together and strong enough to say, "Hey, you can't fucking say that to us. Fuck you. You'll be there tomorrow, and you'd better be on the fucking stage." Because all he needed was a good kick in his fucking pants and he would have made it. But the fact that they [Johnny and Jerry] were itchy, and all the circumstances that brought us to our *death*, you know....

But on that last moment there, where he comes down and says "Man I love this new band, Sylvain," he was kind of saying, "Thanks for all the good stuff." I would hear it from a lot of people, that he said to them, "Sylvain taught me everything I know." What a fucking compliment.

Bob Dylan said that he wished he wrote "You Can't Put Your Arms Round A Memory." *Bob Dylan?*

I mean, what more can you fucking say?

FROM *Mona et moi*

DANNY GARCIA started his career writing for Spanish music magazines in the 1990s and has contributed to a number of publications, including the notorious magazine *High Times*. By the early 2000s, Garcia was already writing, directing and producing a series of short documentaries for BTV, Barcelona's local TV station. In 2012, Garcia directed *The Rise and Fall of The Clash*, a controversial film dealing with the obscure end of The Clash. In 2014, *Looking for Johnny*, Garcia's documentary on the legendary New York Dolls guitarist Johnny Thunders, was released worldwide. *Looking for Johnny* reached Number 10 in the *Billboard* Music Video chart in the US, and Number 1 in Sweden and Japan. In 2016, after a successful film festival run, *Sad Vacation*, his documentary on Sid and Nancy, was also released worldwide. He is currently at work on a new music documentary on Stiv Bators.

This book contains edited extracts from the original transcripts of the interviews conducted for the documentary *Looking for Johnny*. Interviewees include Sylvain Sylvain, Walter Lure, Leee Black Childers, Billy Rath, Marty Thau, Lenny Kaye, Peter Perrett, Bob Gruen, Gail Higgins, Richard Lloyd, John Perry, Rick Rivets, Sami Yaffa, Terry Chimes, Frank Infante, Andy Shernoff, Peter Jordan, Stevie Klasson, BP Fallon, Alison Gordy, Nina Antonia, Neal X, Luigi Scorcia, Marcia Resnick, Barry Jones, Nite Bob, Cynthia Ross, Rachel Amodeo, Phyllis Stein, Steve Hooker, Simon Ritt, Linda Falzarano, Howie Pyro, Jill Wisoff, and Peter Orr.

Extra special thanks to Stevie Klasson, Kim Montenegro, Nina Antonia, Leee Black Childers (RIP), Phyllis Stein, Courtney Stein, Marcia Resnick, Yann Mercader (RIP), Xavi Mercader, Kathy Findlay, Cody Smyth, Daisy Wake, Kathy Friery, Linda Falzarano, Henri Paul Tortosa, Simon Ritt, Nacho Costa, Johnny Douglas, Rory Cain, César Méndez, Jeff Joseph, Rudy Fernández, Vanessa D'Amelio, Xavi Mercadé, Sergi Garcia, Iris Berry, and everybody who helped us in the making of *Looking for Johnny*. This book is for you.

ALSO FROM PUNK HOSTAGE PRESS

Fractured by Danny Baker

The Daughters of Bastards by Iris Berry

Impress by C.V. Auchterlonie

Tomorrow, Yvonne–Poetry & Prose For Suicidal Egotists
by Yvonne De la Vega

Miracles of the Blog: A Series
by Carolyn Srygley-Moore

8th & Agony by Rich Ferguson

Moth Wing Tea by Dennis Cruz

Showgirl Confidential by Pleasant Gehman

Blood Music by Frank Reardon

History of Broken Love Things by SB Stokes

Yeah, Well… by Joel Landmine

Dreams Gone Mad With Hope by S.A. Griffin

How to Take a Bullet and Other Survival Poems
by Hollie Hardy

Dead Lions by A.D. Winans

Scars by Nadia Bruce Rawlings

Stealing the Midnight From a Handful of Days
by Michele McDannold

Thugness Is a Virtue by Hannah Wehr

When I Was a Dynamiter, or, How a Nice Catholic Boy Became a Merry Prankster, a Pornographer, and a Bridegroom Seven Times by Lee Quarnstrom

Introvert/Extrovert by Russell Jaffe

No Greater Love by Die Dragonetti

No Parachutes to Carry Me Home by Maisha Z Johnson

#1 Son and Other Stories by Michael Marcus

By Jack Grisham
Untamed
Code Blue: A Love Story

By Alexandra Naughton
I Will Always Be Your Whore/Love Songs for Billy Corgan
You Could Never Objectify Me More Than I've Already Objectified Myself

By A. Razor
Better Than a Gun in a Knife Fight
Drawn Blood: Collected Works From D.B.P. Ltd., 1985-1995
Beaten Up Beaten Down
Small Catastrophes in a Big World
Half-Century Status
Days of Xmas Poems

CPSIA information can be obtained
at www.ICGtesting.com
Printed in the USA
LVHW111617170419
614532LV00002B/226/P

9 781940 213033